GOOD NIGHT, SLEEP TIGHT

To our editor,
Jane Burnard

Thanks also to the staff of Wellington Library, Shropshire, England

Scholastic Children's Books,
Commonwealth House, 1-19 New Oxford Street
London WC1A 1NU, UK
a division of Scholastic Ltd
London ~ New York ~ Toronto ~ Sydney ~ Auckland
Mexico City ~ New Delhi ~ Hong Kong

Published in the UK by Scholastic Ltd, 2000

ISBN 0 439 01222 8

Printed and bound in Germany

2 4 6 8 10 9 7 5 3 1

GOOD NIGHT, SLEEP TIGHT

A poem for every night of the year!

366 POEMS TO BRING YOU THE SWEETEST OF DREAMS

Compiled by

 Ivan and Mal Jones

SCHOLASTIC
PRESS

CONTENTS

CONTENTS

5

CONTENTS

JANUARY
1st – 31st

Sleep is like
Snowflakes
Gentle and calm...

1st

The Tiny Little Rocket

New Year's Day

There's a tiny little rocket
that will take you to the stars
It only flies there once a year
but zips you out past Mars

Its fins are solid silver
with a door made out of gold
there's a cosy pilot seat inside
for a person young or old

It whizzes out to deepest space
while you hold on by the handle
and there you'll find the golden sun
our ever burning candle

There's a button in the rocket
that winks just by your head
and you have to press that button
when it turns from green to red

You press the button with your
    thumb
and a banner is unfurled
it stretches from the moon to Mars
saying "Happy Birthday World"

David Fickling

2nd

Recipe For a Good Night's Sleep

Ingredients:
One child (about 20 kg.)
A pair of pyjamas
Two heavy eyelids
Several teddies
Picture books (to taste)
A handful of yawns

Method:
First heat the bed to the correct
    temperature.
Place the filling in the pyjamas.
Add the rest of the ingredients and
    sprinkle with yawns.
Put the mixture into the pre-
    warmed bed.
Lower the light and leave for several
    hours.
If well done, the child will rise
    nicely.
Turn out on the right side of the
    bed.

Sue Cowling

3rd

My List of Promises

On New Year's Day
I made a list
of things I'd try to do.
It was my list
of promises to keep
the whole year through.

"I will not shout.
I will not spit.
I'll eat up all my greens.
I'll read a book.
I won't tell lies.
I'll not wear dirty jeans."

"I'll clean my shoes.
I'll brush my teeth.
I promise not to fight."
The list was long.
It took me most
of New Year's Day to write!

In bed that night
I read my list
before I fell asleep.
Oh, so many,
many promises!
How many will I keep?

Wes Magee

4th

Who Likes Cuddles?

Who likes cuddles?
Me.
Who likes hugs?
Me.

Who likes tickles?
Me.
Who likes getting their face
stroked?
Me.
Who likes being lifted up high?
Me.

Who likes sitting on laps?
Me.
Who likes being whirled round and
round?
Me.

But best of all I like
getting into bed and getting
   blowy blowy
down my neck behind my ear.
A big warm tickly blow
lovely.

Michael Rosen

JANUARY
5th

5th

Jack Frost

The door was shut, as doors
   should be,
Before you went to bed last night;
But Jack Frost has got in, you see,
And left your window silver white.

He must have waited till you slept;
And not a single word he spoke,
But pencilled o'er the panes
   and crept
Away again before you woke.

And now you cannot see the hills
Nor fields that stretch beyond
   the lane;
But there are fairer things
   than these
His fingers traced on every pane.

Rocks and castles towering high;
Hills and dales and streams
   and fields;
And knights in armour riding by,
With nodding plumes and shining
   shields.

And here are little boats, and there
Big ships with sails spread to
   the breeze;
And yonder, palm trees waving fair
On islands set in silver seas.

And butterflies with gauzy wings;
And herds of cows and flocks of
   sheep;
And fruit and flowers and all
   the things
You see when you are sound asleep.

For creeping softly underneath
The door, when all the lights
   are out,
Jack Frost takes every breath you
   breathe
And knows the things you think
about.

He paints them on the window
   pane,
In fairy lines with frozen steam;
And when you wake you see again
The lovely things you saw in
   dream.

Gabriel Setoun

11

6th

Furry Bear

If I were a bear
And a big bear too,
I shouldn't much care
If it froze or snew;
I shouldn't much mind
If it snowed or friz –
I'd be all fur-lined
With a coat like his!

For I'd have fur boots and a brown
    fur wrap,
And brown fur knickers and a big
    fur cap.
I'd have a fur muffle-ruff to cover
    my jaws,
And brown fur mittens on my big
    brown paws.
With a big brown furry-down up to
    my head,
I'd sleep all winter in a big fur bed.

A.A. Milne

7th

The Folk Who Live in Backward Town

The folk who live in Backward
    Town
Are inside out and upside down.
They wear their hats inside their
    heads
And go to sleep beneath their beds.
They only eat the apple peeling
And take their walks across the
    ceiling.

Mary Ann Hoberman

8th

Cats

Cats sleep
Anywhere,
Any table,
Any chair,
Top of piano,
Window-ledge,
In the middle,
On the edge,
Open drawer,
Empty shoe,
Anybody's
Lap will do,
Fitted in a
Cardboard box,
In the cupboard
With your frocks –
Anywhere!
They don't care!
Cats sleep
Anywhere.

Eleanor Farjeon

9th

Mrs Moon

Mrs Moon
sitting up in the sky
little old Lady
rock-a-bye
with a ball of fading light
and silvery needles
knitting the night

Roger McGough

10th

The Little Griffin Bird

I found an egg and took it home,
I wrapped it up and kept it warm,
I kept it by me all the time,
And never left it on its own.

Dead on the stroke of midnight
When my room was quiet and still,
I heard the eggshell cracking and
A little cheeping trill.

Out of that broken egg there
   hopped
A little griffin bird,
He whimpered as he spoke to me
And this is what I heard:

"I want my Mummy and I want her
   NOW!"

A tiny golden griffin bird
With feathers damp and tail curled
   tight
He put his head under his wing
And cried as though he'd cry all
   night:

"I want my Mummy and I want her
   NOW!"

"Well, keep your feathers on,"
   I said,
"And don't get all upset,
She's probably on her way right
   now,
She'll be here soon, I bet."

I heard a mighty whooshing sound
Of feathers, wings and beak
And tearing down out of the sky,
Shrieking a griffin shriek

In at my bedroom window
That mother griffin flew.
"Darling!" she squawked. "My
   precious chick!
At last, at last I've found you!"

She squeezed in underneath my bed
And snoodled up her child,
They chirped and cooed and
   chirruped
They billed and cooed and smiled.

Then away they flew together
To the place where griffins live,
Calling: "Bless you! Thank you!"
   and "Goodbye!"
They were happy. So was I.

Henrietta Branford

11th

Five Little Puppies

Five little puppies
Lying in a heap,
Five little puppies
All fast asleep.
One's called Pop –
He's full of fizz;
Two's called Nosy –
Because she is;
Three and four
Are Dot and Spot,
And five is Flipper:
That's the lot.

Five little puppies,
All flopped about,
All fast asleep,
All crashed out.

Eric Finney

12th

Young Night Thought

All night long, and every night,
When my mamma puts out the
    light,
I see the people marching by,
As plain as day, before my eye.

Armies and emperors and kings,
All carrying different kinds of
    things,
And marching in so grand a way,
You never saw the like by day.

So fine a show was never seen
At the great circus on the green;
For every kind of beast and man
Is marching in that caravan.

At first they move a little slow,
But still the faster on they go,
And still beside them close I keep
Until we reach the town of Sleep.

Robert Louis Stevenson

13th

Sleeping in School

Every morning, Mum wakes me up
But I'm tired, I like my bed
Down at breakfast
I fall asleep in my Weetabix
In the car
I fall asleep in my school bag
On the playground
I fall asleep on the football
In the classroom
I fall asleep in my maths book
In the dinner hall
I fall asleep in my salad

Time to go to bed
The end of a long day
Everyone's asleep
But I just want to play.

Joshua Feehan (7)

14th

Rack-A-Bye, Baby

Rack-a-bye, baby,
    pon tap a tree tap,
Wen de win blow
    de crib a go swing;
Wen de lim bruck
    de crib a go drap,
Den lim, crib, an baby,
    eberyting drap. BRAP!

Traditional West Indian

15th

All Night

Although it's night,
I think I might
Creep out of bed
And poke my head
Round Mummy's door –
Hear Daddy snore!
And if I snuggle,
Diggle, duggle,
I think they may,
I think they might,
Let me stay
With them – all night!

Tony Bradman

16th

Past Three O'Clock
(Song of the Watchmen)

Past three o'clock,
And a cold frosty morning:
Past three o'clock,
Good morrow masters all.

While in your beds you're
   peacefully sleeping,
Under the stars our watch we are
   keeping.

We go the round, you rest at your
   leisure,
Safe is your house and safe is your
   treasure.

When morning breaks, and
   slumber is ended,
Give us your thanks, your homes
   we've defended.

Past three o'clock,
And a cold frosty morning:
Past three o'clock,
Good morrow masters all.

James Fortescue

17th

Wynken, Blynken and Nod

Wynken, Blynken, and Nod one
   night
Sailed off in a wooden shoe –
Sailed on a river of crystal light,
Into a sea of dew.
"Where are you going, and what do
   you wish?"
The old moon asked the three.
"We have come to fish for the
   herring fish
That live in this beautiful sea;
Nets of silver and gold have we!"
    Said Wynken,
    Blynken,
    And Nod.

The old moon laughed and sang a
   song,
As they rocked in the wooden shoe,
And the wind that sped them all
   night long
Ruffled the waves of dew.
The little stars were the herring
   fish
That lived in that beautiful sea –
"Now cast your nets wherever you
   wish –
Never afeard are we,"
So cried the stars to the fishermen
   three:
    Wynken,
    Blynken,
    And Nod.

All night long their nets they
   threw
To the stars in the twinkling foam –
Then down from the skies came the
   wooden shoe,
Bringing the fishermen home;
'Twas all so pretty a sail it seemed
As if it could not be,
And some folks thought 'twas a
   dream they'd dreamed
Of sailing that beautiful sea –
But I shall name you the fishermen
   three:
      Wynken,
      Blynken,
      And Nod.

Wynken and Blynken are two little
   eyes,
And Nod is a little head,
And the wooden shoe that sailed
   the skies
Is the wee one's trundle-bed.
So shut your eyes while Mother
   sings
Of wonderful sights that be,
And you shall see the beautiful
   things
As you rock in the misty sea,
Where the old shoe rocked the
   fishermen three:
      Wynken,
      Blynken,
      And Nod.

Eugene Field

18th

Communications

I'll read to you.
THE SUN IS IN THE WEST.
THE EAST IS VERY OLD.
MY HOME IS BEST.

I'll write to you.
I'll write about the sky
The sun the moon the stars
And satellites that fly
The thousand things there are
And why...

I'll talk to you.
I'll tell you all my things.
My guinea pig had quins.
And swallows when they fly
Have metal wings.
Such curves and caperings!
You seem to see their smoke trails
    overhead.

The puppy made a mess on
    Granma's bed.

And even people die.

I don't know what I said.

I'll sing to you.
The blackbird in the lane
Is singing too.
I'll sing again, again,
For me and you
And when the world is done
And everyone is gone
I'll still sing on.

Ursula Moray Williams

20th

The Snowstorm

Heave-ho,
Buckets of snow,
The giant is combing his beard.
The snow is as high
As the top of the sky,
And the world has disappeared.

Dennis Lee

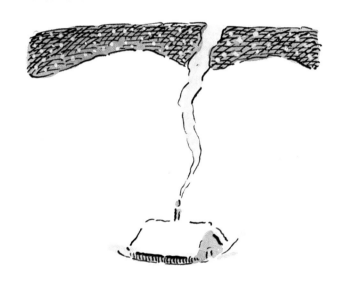

19th

My Bed

My bed is like a little boat
floating out to sea.
And now it's like an island
with a coconut tree.

My bed is like a racing car
roaring in a race,
And now it's like a rocket
rising into space.

My bed is like a submarine
diving down deep.
And now my bed is just a bed
because I'm fast asleep.

Tony Mitton

JANUARY
21st

 21st

Upon the Hearth the Fire is Red

Upon the hearth the fire is red,
Beneath the roof there is a bed
But not yet weary are our feet,
Still round the corner we may meet
A sudden tree or standing stone
That none have seen but we alone.

Tree and flower and leaf and grass,
Let them pass! Let them pass!
Hill and water under sky,
Pass them by! Pass them by!

Still round the corner there may
    wait
A new road or a secret gate,
And though we pass them by today,
Tomorrow we may come this way
And take the hidden paths that run
Towards the moon or to the sun.

Apple, thorn and nut and sloe,
Let them go! Let them go!
Sand and stone and pool and dell,
Fare you well! Fare you well!

Home is behind, the world ahead,
And there are many paths to tread
Through shadows to the edge of
    night,
Until the stars are all alight.
Then world behind and home
    ahead,
We'll wander back to home and
    bed.

Mist and twilight, cloud and shade,
Away shall fade! Away shall fade!
Fire and lamp, and meat and bread,
And then to bed! And then to bed!

J.R.R. Tolkien

22nd

Books at Bedtime

Here a wizard casts a spell.
Here big giants roar and yell.
  Here are rabbits having fun.
  Here's an island in the sun.
Here the tortoise wins the race.
Here's a rocket lost in space.
  Here are children on a beach.
  Here's a magic, flying peach.
Here green monsters come and go.
Here's old Santa in the snow.
  Here's the wolf at Grandma's
    door.
  Eleven books piled on the floor.

Wes Magee

23rd

Moon

"The moon is thousands of miles
  away,"
My Uncle Trevor said.
Why can't he see
It's caught in a tree
Above our onion bed?

Gareth Owen

24th

Chinese New Year

Dragon

Dragon, dragon
with your bright
fierce and fiery
eye –
can I touch
your scaly skin
as you ramble
by?

Dragon, dragon,
when your tail
swishes
to and fro –
shall I feel
your burning breath
in the lantern's
glow?

"Jade and silver,
gold and red –
touch me
if you dare!
I am bringing
NEW YEAR in
with magic
everywhere!"

Jean Kenward

25th

Burns Night

Over the Sky to See

Sherp starlight spikes through
    thinnest cloud
    on a mountain dark an' high,
whaur deep-coat sheep bleat lang
    and loud
    when a hauf moon sclims in a
Scottish sky.

A grey seal bobs on a glassy loch,
    the seaburds wheel an' fly.
The fisher boats ignore the clock
    when a hauf moon skelps in a
Scottish sky.

The burnies gush frae glen an' brae
    tae join the torrent's cry.
The heather's colour is darker still
    when a hauf moon skirls in a
Scottish sky.

John Rice

burnies = small streams.
brae = hill

24

26th

Willie Winkie

Wee Willie Winkie runs through
   the town,
Upstairs and downstairs in his
   night-gown,
Rapping at the window, crying at
   the lock,
"Are the children all in bed, it's
   past ten o'clock?"

"Hey, Willie Winkie, are you
   coming in?
The cat's winding bits of thread
   round the sleeping hen,
The dog's stretched on the floor
   and doesn't give a cheep,
But here's a wakeful laddie, that
   just won't fall asleep."

Anything but sleep, you rogue!
   glowering like the moon,
Rattling in an iron jug with an iron
   spoon,
Rumbling, tumbling round about,
   crowing like a cock,
Shrieking like I don't know what,
   waking sleeping folk.

Wee Willie Winkie runs through
   the town,
Upstairs and downstairs in his
   night-gown,
Rapping at the window, crying at
   the lock,
"Are the children all in bed, it's
   past ten o'clock?"

William Miller
(adapted from Scots by Mal Lewis Jones)

27th

Glow-in-the-Dark Bedroom

I have glow-in-the-dark curtains
With glow-in-the-dark cars
And, stuck all over the ceiling,
Glow-in-the-dark stars.

My glow-in-the-dark slippers
Are grinning beside my bed,
And there sits my teddy
With his glow-in-the-dark head.

I'm sick and tired of counting
Glow-in-the-dark sheep:
Their shimmering and shining
Won't get me off to sleep.

They can all glow on without me,
If anybody cares,
I've found a no-glow area:
I'm sleeping under the stairs!

Celia Warren

28th

In the Bath

In the bath I like to wonder
which things float and which go
    under.
I can float things made of wood
But Mummy's handbag's not so
    good.

My toy boat will sail around
but Daddy's watch goes gurgling
    down.
You can often float a welly
but not the zapper for the telly.

With things that float I often find
I play and no one seems to mind.
But people can get quite annoyant
when I play with things
    non-buoyant.

Kjartan Poskitt

29th

Babe-in-the-Moon

The man-in-the-moon had a baby
   Sing, stars, sing
Tubby and white, and
  magically bright
   Sing, stars, sing

And when the moon was a crescent
   Sing, stars, sing
He rocked his baby to and fro
In his glittering, silver sling.

And when the moon was glowing
  full
   Sing, stars, sing
He played with his baby, swirling
  her giddily
Round and round on a string.

Oh, how the baby chuckled and
  laughed!
   Sing, stars, sing
The happiest babe in the whole
  universe
   Sing, stars, sing

Patricia Leighton

30th

The Happy Hedgehogs

The happiness of hedgehogs
   Lies in complete repose.
They spend the months of winter
   In a long delicious doze;
And if they note the time at all
   They think "How fast it goes!"

E.V. Rieu

31st

Sleep is Like Snowflakes

Sleep is like
Snowflakes
Gentle and calm.
Sleep is like
Sunshine
Warm as balm.
Sleep is like
Rose petals
Fragrant and sweet.
Sleep is like
Magic
Dreamy and deep.
Sleep makes you
Feel good
From your head
To your toes
But why
It does so
Nobody knows.

Ivan Jones

FEBRUARY
1st – 29th

Hush! I'll show you quiet things –
moon and stars and a barn owl's wings...

FEBRUARY
1st & 2nd

Mum Reads to Me Every Night

Mum reads to me every night

she's reading "The Tailor of
    Gloucester"

she sits on the edge of the bed
and reads in a sing-song voice
that drifts on forever

I tell her
her voice is sleepy
and she gets all huffy
and says,
well, I shan't bother then
what a thing to say
really
I don't think I'll bother.

"Sleepy"
was how I liked it
I wasn't complaining.

Michael Rosen

Teddydums in Bed

I lay down with my Teddydums
And held his little nose
I sucked his ear and stroked his
    paws
And then his furry toes.

Teddydums lay quietly
He didn't mind one bit
He lay there smiling silently
His ear soaked in my spit!

"Teddydums," I said to him,
"You must be thinking deep,
Or could it be that unlike me,
You are fast asleep?"

Ivan Jones

3rd

Snow-Lady

Snow-lady, snow-lady,
Out there in the cold
With your fat carrot-nose
And your buttons of gold;
The hat on your head
Has a snow-ribbon band
And a robin has perched
On your ice-stiffened hand.

Snow-lady, snow-lady
Please don't go away!
We'll build a tall snowman
Beside you today.
Then you won't feel lonely
Out there in the night,
With the moon shining down
And the frosty starlight.

Mary Dawson-Jeffries

4th

When You Close those Tired Eyes

Step aboard the ship of dreams
Board the galleon of rhyme
Sail upon all seven seas
And travel to the end of time.

Meet with dragons in their caves
Rescue princes from tall towers
With dolphins surf the waves
And chat with whales for hours.

Find pirate treasure buried deep
Soar with condors in the skies
All this may happen as you sleep,
When you close those tired eyes.

Jim Hatfield

5th

Just for Fun

Just for fun
We picked on the sun
And called her Yellowhead!

So she ran away
With her friend Miss Day
And we were stuck with Night
instead.

Andrew Fusek Peters

6th

Corroboree

The clap, clap, clap of the clap-
    sticks beat
By the old, red rocks with their
    scars
To the stamp, stamp, stamp of the
    old men's feet
And the wink, wink, wink of the
    stars.
With the drone, drone, drone of the
    didgeridoo
And the sound of its ancient tune
In the dance of the snake and the
    kangaroo
By the light of the walkabout
    moon.
The chants will rise and drift and
    fall
While the night with a magic fills
Where the old men dance to the
    Dreamtime's call
In the heart of the secret hills.

Max Fatchen

*Corroboree is a dance performed at
festivals by the aborigines of Australia,
accompanied by the music of the
didgeridoo*

7th

8th

The Train Pulled in the Station

O, the train pulled in the station,
　　The bell was ringing wet;
The track ran by the depot,
　　And I think it's running yet.

'Twas midnight on the ocean,
　　Not a streetcar was in sight;
The sun and moon were shining,
　　And it rained all day that night.

'Twas a summer day in winter,
　　And the snow was raining fast;
As a barefoot boy, with shoes on,
　　Stood, sitting on the grass.

O, I jumped into the river,
　　Just because it had a bed;
I took a sheet of water
　　For to cover up my head.

American Folk Song

Good Company

I sleep in a room at the top of the
　　house
With a flea, and a fly, and a soft-
　　scratching mouse,
And a spider that hangs by a thread
　　from the ceiling,
Who gives me each day such a
　　curious feeling
When I watch him at work on his
　　beautiful weave
Of his web that's so fine I can
　　hardly believe
It won't all end up in such terrible
　　tangles,
For he sways as he weaves, and
　　spins as he dangles.
I cannot get up to that spider, I know,
And hope he won't get down to me
　　here below,
And yet when I wake in the chill
　　morning air
I'd miss him if he were not still
　　swinging there,
For I have in my room such good
　　company,
There's him, and the mouse, and the
　　fly, and the flea.

Leonard Clark

33

9th

Bananas

Bananas,
In pyjamas,
Are coming down the stairs;
Bananas,
In pyjamas,
Are coming down in pairs;
Bananas,
In pyjamas,
Are chasing teddy bears –
'Cos on Tuesdays
They all try to
CATCH THEM UNAWARES.

Carey Blyton

10th

Sleeping

One............that's you asleep in bed.
Two...........soft pillows for your
                    head.
Three.........books lying on the floor.
Four...........shoes by the bedroom
                    door.
Five............old teds beside you lie.
Six.............stars twinkle in the sky.
Seven.........spiders spin all night.
Eight.........hours till the dawn's
                    first light.
Nine...........mice in the darkness
                    creep.
Ten............angels watch you while
                    you sleep.

Wes Magee

11th

Sleeping Beauty

Fair Rosa was a lovely girl,
  A lovely girl, a lovely girl,
Fair Rosa was a lovely girl,
  Lived long, long ago.

She lived up in a great high tower,
  A great high tower, a great
  high tower,
She lived up in a great high tower,
  Long, long ago.

A wicked fairy cast her spell,
  Cast her spell, cast her spell,
A wicked fairy cast her spell,
  Long, long ago.

Fair Rosa slept for a hundred years,
  A hundred years, a hundred
  years,
Fair Rosa slept for a hundred years,
  Long, long ago.

A briar hedge grew all around,
  All around, all around,
A briar hedge grew all around,
  Long, long ago.

A handsome prince came riding by,
  Riding by, riding by,
A handsome prince came riding by,
  Long, long ago.

He chopped the hedge down with
  his sword,
  With his sword, with his sword,
He chopped the hedge down with
  his sword,
  Long, long ago.

He woke Fair Rosa with a kiss,
  With a kiss, with a kiss,
He woke Fair Rosa with a kiss,
  Long, long ago.

And now she's happy as a bride,
  As a bride, as a bride,
And now she's happy as a bride,
  Long, long ago.

Traditional

35

12th

You Be Saucer

You be saucer,
I'll be cup,
piggyback, piggyback,
pick me up.

You be tree,
I'll be pears,
carry me, carry me
up the stairs.

You be Good,
I'll be Night,
tuck me in, tuck me in
nice and tight.

Eve Merriam

13th

Into the Bathtub

Into the bathtub,
Great big splosh.
Toes in the bathtub,
Toes in the wash.

Soap's very slidy,
Soap smells sweet.
Soap all over,
Soap on your feet.

Rinse all the soap off,
Dirt floats away.
Dirt in the water.
Water's gone grey.

Out of the bathtub,
Glug, glug, glug.
Great big towel,
Great big hug.

Wendy Cope

FEBRUARY
14th & 15th

Valentine's Day

I've Taken to My Bed

I've taken to my bed
(And my bed has taken to me)
We're getting married in the
    spring
How happy we shall be

We'll raise lots of little bunks
A sleeping-bag or two
Take my advice: find a bed that's
    nice
Lie down and say: "I love you".

Roger McGough

The Land of Counterpane

When I was sick and lay a-bed,
I had two pillows at my head,
And all my toys beside me lay
To keep me happy all the day.

And sometimes for an hour or so
I watched my leaden soldiers go,
With different uniforms and drills,
Among the bed-clothes, through
    the hills;

And sometimes sent my ships in
    fleets
All up and down among the sheets;
Or brought my trees and houses
    out,
And planted cities all about.

I was the giant great and still
That sits upon the pillow-hill,
And sees before him, dale and
    plain,
The pleasant land of counterpane.

Robert Louis Stevenson

16th

Quiet Things

Hush! I'll show you quiet things –
moon and stars and a barn owl's
  wings
speckled moth on mottled sill
white mare standing paper-still
gap-toothed gravestones,
  hollow trees
flat-roofed fungus colonies
coins and bones long buried deep
hedgehog hunched in spiny sleep.

Sue Cowling

17th

from **The Camel's Complaint**

Cats, you're aware, can repose in a
  chair,
  Chickens can roost upon rails;
Puppies are able to sleep in a
  stable,
  And oysters can slumber in pails.
    But no one supposes
    A poor camel dozes –
    Any place does for me.

Lambs are enclosed where it's
  never exposed,
  Coops are constructed for hens;
Kittens are treated to houses well
  heated.
  And pigs are protected by pens.
    But a camel comes handy
    Wherever it's sandy –
    Anywhere does for me.

Charles E. Carryl

18th

Night Sounds

When I lie in bed
I think I can hear
The stars being switched on
I think I can.

And I think I can hear
The moon
Breathing.

But I have to be still.
So still.
All the house is sleeping.
Except for me.

Then I think I can hear it.

Berlie Doherty

19th

Deep Peace of the Running Wave

Deep peace of the Running Wave to
 you.
Deep peace of the Flowing Air to
 you.
Deep peace of the Quiet Earth to
 you.
Deep peace of the Shining Stars to
 you.
Deep peace of the Son of Peace to
 you.

Celtic Benediction

20th

Hovercrafts

On the quiet midnight hour,
Pyjamas and hovercrafts fill the
    sky,
In village and city they take off
    from beds,
One then another, it's time to fly.

Some are small as a fluffed-up
    pillow
Others, as big as a king-sized bed,
Without the slightest need of gas,
Their engines are on feathers fed.

No sooner is the light switched off,
Pyjama passengers sigh *Good*
    night!
The hovercraft rises silent and soft,
The tour has begun, now hold on
    tight!

The journey ends with the
    hovering of dawn
Out of the night and into the day,
They make a perfect bedroom
    landing,
Leave their passengers and fly
    away.

If you are lucky, at the edge of the
    bed,
You might just find a tiny feather
The hovercraft dropped on its
    return
In a dream of stormy weather.

Wanda Chotomska
Translated by Leszek Girtler and
Andrew Fusek Peters

21st

The Waltzing Polar Bears

While the snowy owl hoots and the
   Arctic fox wails,
The polar bear waltzes
In white tie and tails.

His top hat gets tilted as he spins
   around twice,
His long claws go rattling
Over the ice.

The Northern Lights up in the
   heavens glow down
As his partner appears
In a shimmering gown.

Reflected in glaciers, they dance
   jaw-to-jaw
Through the hail and the blizzard
And the hurricane's roar.

He wheels her around on her
   sparkling slippers
While the seals and penguins
Applaud with their flippers.

And squawk in amazement and
   bark with delight
At the polar bears waltzing
Through the long Arctic night.

Andrew Matthews

22nd

The Toys' Playtime

When *we* go to bed at the end of
    the day,
our toys wake up and start to play.

They wait until we're fast asleep,
then *they* come alive and out they
    creep.

The ball goes bouncing. The doll
    does a dance.
The little ponies preen and prance.

The toy car roars across the room.
The rocket starts to take off:
    ZOOM!

The robot reads a picture book,
then teddy comes and takes a look.

And all the time we're sleeping
    tight,
the toys are playing through the
    night.

But when the sunlight warms our
    faces,
the toys sit quietly in their places.

They do not move. They make no
    noise.
You don't fool us, you naughty
    toys!

Tony Mitton

23rd

The Night will Never Stay

The night will never stay,
The night will still go by,
Though with a million stars
You pin it to the sky;
Though you bind it with the
    blowing wind
And buckle it with the moon,
The night will slip away
Like sorrow or a tune.

Eleanor Farjeon

24th

On Nights when Hail

On nights when hail
falls noisily
on bamboo leaves,
I completely hate
to sleep alone.

Izumi Shikibu
Translated by Willis Barnstone

25th

The North Wind Doth Blow

The North Wind doth blow
And we shall have snow
And what will poor robin do then,
    poor thing?
He'll sit in a barn
And keep himself warm
And hide his head under his wing,
    poor thing.

Anon

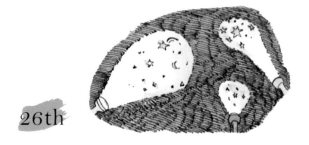

A Day in the Life of Danny the Cat

Danny wakes up
Eats
finds a private place in the garden,
He returns
Plays with the plants
And sleeps.
Danny wakes up
Eats
Inspects the garden
Finds a cosy place
And sleeps.
Danny wakes up
Comes indoors
Inspects the carpet
Scratches himself
And sleeps.

Torches at Night

It is the torches I remember best.
Going home on a winter's evening
We would point them skyward,
Screwing the fronts to sharpen the
    pencils of light
That they might pierce the
    darkness the better.
Bold young challengers of stars
We competed in length and
    brightness.
Yes, better than the chips,
Tart with vinegar and salt grains,
In bags like small grease-proof
    hats,
Better even than the large orange
    bottles,
Tizer tasting of fruit that never
    was,
Were the torches,
Their beams like friendly knives
Making cuts in a darkness
Which oh so quickly healed
At the touch of a switch.

John Cotton

Danny wakes up
Goes in the garden
Over the fence
Has a fight with Ginger
Makes a date with Sandy
Climbs on to next door's shed
And sleeps.
Danny wakes up
Comes indoors
Rubs up the chair leg
Rubs up a human leg
Sharpens his claws
On a human leg
Eats
And sleeps.

Danny wakes up
Eats
Watches a nature programme
Finds a private place in the garden,
Finds Sandy in next door's garden
Next door's dog finds Danny
Sandy runs north
Danny runs home
Eats and sleeps.
Danny wakes up
Checks for mice
Checks for birds
Checks for dogs
Checks for food
Finds a private place in the garden
Eats
And sleeps.

Danny has hobbies,
Being stroked
Car watching
And smelling feet
He loves life,
Keeps fit
And keeps clean,
Every night he covers himself
In spit,
Then he eats
And sleeps.

Benjamin Zephaniah

28th

The Satellite Circus

In winter's sharp dark
  as the clouds speed and fly,
the Satellite Circus
  arrives in the sky.

And dressed in the sparkle
  of diamond and crown,
the Satellite Circus
  lets the planets play clown.

An acrobat troupe
  bounding skywards so fast,
the Satellite Circus
  presents a star cast.

High in this big top
  the trapeze sways in time,
the Satellite Circus
  performs a moon-mime.

To the music of midnight
  the shooting stars dance,
the Satellite Circus
  has us Earthlings in trance.

John Rice

29th
Leap Year

Kangaroo – Kangaroo!

The kangaroo of Australia
Lives on the burning plain,
He keeps on leaping in the air
'Cos it's hot when he lands again.

Spike Milligan

MARCH
1st – 31st

I'll rock you away to that Sugar-Plum Tree
In the garden of Shut-Eye Town...

1st

St David's Day

I Wear a Daffodil on David's Day

The spring is late this year.
No daffodils for David's Day.
I had to wear a little plastic one.
Mr Morgan has a little leek made
   out of felt.
He wears it every year.
He says that David's an example to
   us all –
A Prince of Cardigan who became a
   priest.
I don't know much about him
   though,
Except he was a prince's son and
   holy man
And that I wear a daffodil on
   David's Day
And feel a bit more Welsh.

Kevin Bamford

2nd

Snuggles

Work done
for the day
the sun
switches on
the moon
pulls
the clouds
over its
head and
snuggles
right down
into the
cosy bottom
of the sky.

Roger McGough

3rd

Life as a Sheep

Sometimes
Oi stands
Sometimes
Oi sits
Then
Stands again
Then
Sits
For a bit.

Sometimes
Oi wanders
Sometimes
Oi stays
Sometimes
Oi chews
Sometimes
Oi strays.

Sometimes
Oi coughs
Sometimes
Oi don't
Sometimes
Oi bleats
Sometimes
Oi won't.
Sometimes
Oi watch

The human race
Or
Smiles to meself
Or
Stares into space.

And when
Oi's happy
Oi'd dance and sing
But Oi
Don't have the knack
To do
Such a thing.

At night
Oi lays
By the old church steeple
And
Falls asleep
By counting people.

Gareth Owen

4th

Up the Wooden Hill

When the clock said eight
A voice boomed, TIME!
And up the wooden hill
I started to climb.

There were slippery screes
And jutting-out crags
But I got to the top
Without any snags.

Across snow-capped peaks
I scrambled, and crashed
Into a mountain pool
Where I plunged and splashed.

I dried myself
And drank from the spring
Water so minty-fresh
It left my teeth tingling.

I entered a cave
Half-dark, half-aglow.
It was warm and snug
Away from the snow.

Into fleecy lambswool
I snuggled down deep,
My mountain-climb over,
I dropped off to sleep.

Ivan Jones

MARCH
5th

 5th

I Like to Stay Up

I like to stay up
and listen
when big people talking
jumbie stories

I does feel
so tingly and excited
inside me

But when my mother say
"Girl, time for bed"

Then is when
I does feel a dread

Then is when
I does cover up
from me feet to me head

Then is when
I does wish I didn't listen
to no stupid jumbie story

Then is when
I does wish I did read
me book instead

Grace Nichols

Jumbie = Guyanese word for ghost

6th

Exactly Like a "V"

When my brother Tommy
Sleeps in bed with me
He doubles up
And makes
himself
exactly
like
a
V

And 'cause the bed is not so wide
A part of him is on my side.

Abram Bunn Ross

7th

A Chill

What can lambkins do
All the keen night through?
Nestle by their woolly mother,
The careful ewe.

What can nestlings do
In the nightly dew?
Sleep beneath their mother's
  wing
Till day breaks anew.

If in field or tree,
There might only be
Such a warm soft sleepy place
Found for me!

Christina Rossetti

8th

Tooth Fairies

Daddy, Daddy,
tell me the truth.
What do the fairies
do with a tooth?

Well, my darling,
who can say
what takes place
beyond the day?

Perhaps they buy
those tiny bones
to carve them into
shining thrones.

Or take each white tooth
safely down
to cut themselves
a gleaming crown.

Perhaps they trim them
square and slick
to build a wall
that's sheer and thick.

Or take up neat
and nimble tools
to shape them into
necklace jewels.

For, dearest daughter,
who can say
what takes place
when we're away
or fast asleep
beyond the day?

Tony Mitton

MARCH
9th

9th

The Dream of a Boy Who Lived at Nine Elms

Nine grenadiers, with bayonets in
  their guns;
Nine bakers' baskets, with hot-
  cross buns;
Nine brown elephants, standing in
  a row;
Nine new velocipedes, good ones to
  go;
Nine knickerbocker suits, with
  buttons all complete;
Nine pair of skates with straps for
  the feet;
Nine clever conjurors eating hot
  coals;
Nine sturdy mountaineers leaping
  on their poles;
Nine little drummer-boys beating
  on their drums;
Nine fat aldermen sitting on their
  thumbs;

Nine new knockers to our front
  door;
Nine new neighbours that I never
  saw before;
Nine times running I dreamt it all
  plain;
With bread and cheese for supper I
  could dream it all again!

William Brighty Rands

velocipedes = early bicycles

10th

The Cat and the Fiddle

Hey diddle diddle,
The cat and the fiddle,
The cow jumped over the moon,
The little dog laughed
To see such fun
And the dish ran away with the
   spoon.

Anon

11th

March Winds

The wind rattles the window frame
and chases milk bottles down
   the path.
It shakes the apple tree outside
   my window
and makes it bang against
   the glass.

Let me in! cries the storm
   but it doesn't bother me at all,
for I am snuggled up in bed,
   cosy, safe and warm.

Jim Hatfield

12th

Curing Song

Your heart is good.
(The Spirit) Shining Darkness will
   be here.
You think only of sad unpleasant
   things,
You are to think of goodness.
Lie down and sleep here.
Shining darkness will join us.
You think of this goodness in your
   dream.
Goodness will be given to you,
I will speak for it, and it will come
   to pass.
It will happen here,
I will ask for your good,
It will happen as I sit by you,
It will be done as I sit here in this
   place.

Yuma Indians, North America

13th

Noah's Trick

Old Noah was a clever man –
He saw the floods a-coming
So he loaded animals into the ark
And set her sails a-running.

BUT

The antelopes were restless
They liked to jump and kick,
The zebras ran and tossed their
 heads
And gave their tails a flick.

The elephants went crazy
And trumpeted alarm,
Hyenas laughed like madmen –
Nothing could make them calm.

The giraffes were very nervous
As they skittered on the deck.
Noah threw his hands up –
"Soon this Ark will be a wreck!"

But the animals just rushed about
And barked or neighed or shrilled
Till Noah said, "I'll count to ten;
Then you *must* be still!"

Old Noah began a-counting,
The only thing to do.
The animals hardly listened
As he said, "One two, one two."

The animals' ears pricked up,
Waiting for number three,
But Noah's voice seemed stuck
In hypnotic harmony.

"One two, one two, one two,"
He went on without a break
Till at last, in the whole of the Ark,
Only Noah stood awake.

Ivan Jones

14th

15th

Invasion

I watched them fall from the sky
one dark, dark night.
Down they came –
hundreds, thousands, millions
of tiny alien shapes –
landing on roofs, walls
gardens and kerbs.

I watched their strange glow
caught in the street lamp
down below.
They trapped my eyes
held them as if by magic.
Soft and slow
round and round
I saw them go.
I watched
  and watched
  and watched
until I fell asleep.

In the morning
all was silent
everywhere white.

Patricia Leighton

Hare, Mr Hare

Hare, Mr Hare,
What is it that makes you hop?
I see the moon of the fifteenth
night
And then I hop
Hoppety hoppety
Hop hop hop.

Japanese Folk Song
Translated by Geoffrey Bownas &
Anthony Thwaite

16th

Sweet Dreams

I wonder as into bed I creep
What it feels like to fall asleep.
I've told myself stories, I've
   counted sheep,
But I'm always asleep when I fall
   asleep.
Tonight my eyes I will open keep,
And I'll stay awake till I fall asleep,
Then I'll know what it feels like to
   fall asleep,
Asleep,
Asleeep,
Asleeeep...

Ogden Nash

17th

St Patrick's Day

Saint Patrick's Night Party

We always have a party
On Saint Patrick's night.
My Granny pins some shamrock
In her hair, so white,
Kay brings treacle toffee
But it's much too hard,
And someone's naughty daughter
Chases chickens in the yard.
Granda plays the fiddle,
Me and Mummy dance a jig,
Swingarounda, swingarounda,
Whirl-i-gig.
Dad drinks lots of Guinness,
And he sings too many songs,
And I never have to go to bed
Till midnight bongs.
So you're welcome to come over –
By the March moonlight
'Cos we always have a party,
A very special party,
Yes we always have a party
On Saint Patrick's night.

Malachy Doyle

18th

Cat on the Rooftop

Meow, said Tabby
As the sun glistened on the big
   tabby cat
And the birds twittered on the
   roof-top-hats.
    Meow, said Tabby,
     Meow

Then the sunshine went far far
   away
And darkness came instead of day.
   The birds all fled
   For the sun had gone
   But Tabby sat there all night long.

The big tabby cat didn't think to
   go to bed,
The stars in the sky glittered in his
   head,
    Meow, said Tabby,
     Meow

As the moon glimmered on the big
   tabby cat
And the stars shimmered on the
   roof-top hats.
    Meow, said Tabby,
     Meow
      Meow
       Meow
        Meow
         Prrrrrrr

Jessie Lewis Jones (11)

19th

Night

Night is a duvet settled down,
the giant black cat's tummy.
Stars are ancient scrolls
telling stories, the moon
is a ball between two stars of
   children;
it watches, trying to keep
its eyes open, so it can
be night and not day.
From my room, I hear
the spit of puddles
as the tyres fray them.

Jenny Kitchener (8)

20th

The Man in the Moon

And the Man in the Moon has a
  boil on his ear –
    Whee!
      Whing!
        What a singular thing!
I know! but these facts are authentic,
  my dear, –
There's a boil on his ear; and a
  corn on his chin –
He calls it a dimple – but dimples
  stick in –
Yet it might be a dimple turned
  over, you know!
  Whang!
  Ho!
      Why, certainly so!
It might be a dimple turned over,
you know!

And the Man in the Moon has a
  rheumatic knee –
  Gee!
    Whizz!
      What a pity that is!
And his toes have worked round
  where his heels ought to be.
So whenever he wants to go North
  he goes *South*,
And comes back with porridge-
  crumbs all round his mouth
And he brushes them off with a
  Japanese fan,
  Whing!
    Whann!
      What a marvellous man!
What a very remarkably
  marvellous man!

J.W. Riley

MARCH
21st & 22nd

21st

At the Riverside Village

My fishing done, I have returned,
 but do not moor my boat;
At the riverside village the moon
 will set just as I go to sleep.
Even if during the night the wind
 wafts me away,
I shall only reach the shallows
 where the rushes bloom.

Ssu-k'ung Shu
Translated by Robert Kotewall and
Norman L. Smith

22nd

Hairwashing

Long or short,
dark or fair,
everyone has to
wash their hair.

Run the water,
fetch shampoo,
make a lather,
oh, boo hoo!

Please don't shriek,
please don't howl,
shut your eyes,
here's the towel.

Brushing's over,
switch off drier:
milk and biscuits
by the fire.

Tony Mitton

23rd

Jemima
(A cautionary tale)

Jemima would not go to bed.
"Sleep's for fools," she always said.
Her dad who dozed both day and
   night
Grumbled loudly, "It's not right!"

But Jemima would not listen,
All night long watched television.
Even when her eyes turned square
The stubborn girl did not care.
Her eyes swelled up, her sight went
   hazy,
Her hair dropped out, her mind
   went crazy.

Jemima's temper went to pot,
She hurled her toys around a lot.
Her school work changed from
   good to bad –
All the teachers cried, "How sad!"

But when Jemima's birthday came
She was too tired to play a game,
At tea she could not stay awake
And crashed face down in her
   birthday cake!
So from this lesson Jemima learned
A good night's sleep should not be
   spurned.

Ivan Jones

24th

Night Train

The train
is a shiny caterpillar
in clackity boots
nosing through the blind night,
munching mile after mile
of darkness.

Irene Rawnsley

25th

From **A Lesson for Mamma**

Dear Mamma, if you just could be
A tiny little girl like me,
And I your mamma, you would see
  How nice I'd be to you.
I'd always let you have your way;
I'd never frown at you and say,
  "You are behaving ill today,
  Such conduct will not do."

I'd buy you candy every day;
I'd go down town with you,
  and say,
"What would my darling like? You
  may
  Have anything you see."
I'd never say, "My pet, you know
'Tis bad for health and teeth, and so
I cannot let you have it. No –
  It would be wrong in me."

I'd never say, "Well, just a *few*!"
I'd let you stop your lessons too;
I'd say, "They are too hard for you,
  Poor child, to understand."
I'd put the books and slates away;
You shouldn't do a thing but play,
And have a party every day.
  Ah-h-h! wouldn't that be grand!

But, Mamma dear, you cannot
  grow
Into a little girl, you know,
And I can't be your mamma; so
  The only thing to do,
Is just for you to try and see
How very, very nice 'twould be
For *you* to do all this for *me*,
  Now, Mamma, *couldn't* you?

Sydney Dayre (Mrs Cochran)

26th

The Story of the Little Woman

There was a little woman,
　　As I have heard tell,
She went to market
　　Her eggs for to sell,
She went to market
　　All on a market day,
And she fell asleep
　　On the King's highway.

There came by a pedlar
　　His name was Stout,
He cut her petticoats
　　All round about;
He cut her petticoats
　　Up to her knees,
Which made the poor woman
　　To shiver and sneeze.

When the little woman
　　Began to awake,
She began to shiver,
　　And she began to shake;
She began to shake,
　　And she began to cry,
Goodness mercy on me,
　　This is none of I!

If it be not I,
　　As I suppose it be,
I have a little dog at home,
　　And he knows me;
If it be I,
　　He'll wag his little tail,
And if it be not I,
　　He'll loudly bark and wail.

Home went the little woman,
　　All in the dark,
Up jumped the little dog,
　　And he began to bark.
He began to bark,
　　And she began to cry,
Goodness mercy on me,
　　I see I be not I!

This poor little woman
    Passed the night on a stile,
She shivered with cold,
    And she trembled the while;
She slept not a wink
    But was all night awake,
And was heartily glad
    When morning did break.

There came by the pedlar
    Returning from town,
She asked him for something
    To match her short gown,
The sly pedlar rogue
    Showed the piece he'd
    purloined,
Said he to the woman,
    It will do nicely joined.

She pinned on the piece,
    And exclaimed, What a match!
I am lucky indeed
    Such a bargain to catch.
The dog wagged his tail,
    And she began to cry,
Goodness mercy on me,
    I've discovered it be I!

Anon

27th

Mrs Brown

As soon as I'm in bed at night
And snugly settled down,
The little girl I am by day
Goes very suddenly away,
And then I'm Mrs Brown.

I have a family of six,
And all of them have names,
The girls are Joyce and Nancy
    Maud,
The boys are Marmaduke and
    Claude
And Percival and James.

We have a house with twenty
    rooms
A mile away from town;
I think it's good for girls and boys
To be allowed to make a noise –
And so does Mr Brown.

We do the most exciting things,
Enough to make you creep;
And on and on and on we go –
I sometimes wonder if I know
When I have gone to sleep.

Rose Fyleman

28th

The Sugar-Plum Tree

Have you ever heard of the Sugar-
　Plum Tree?
　　'Tis a marvel of great renown!
It blooms on the shores of the
　Lollipop sea
　　In the garden of Shut-Eye
　　Town;
The fruit that it bears is so
　wondrously sweet
　　(As those who have tasted it
　　say)
That good little children have only
　to eat
　　Of that fruit to be happy next
　　day.

When you've got to the tree, you
　would have a hard time
　　To capture the fruit which I
　　sing;
The tree is so tall that no person
　could climb
　　To the bough where the sugar-
　　plums swing!
But up in that tree sits a chocolate
　cat,
　　And a gingerbread dog prowls
　　below –
And this is the way you contrive to
　get at
　　Those sugar-plums tempting
　　you so.

You say but the word to that
　gingerbread dog
　　And he barks with such terrible
　　zest
That the chocolate cat is at once all
　agog,
　　As her swelling proportions
　　attest.
And the chocolate cat goes
　cavorting around

From this leafy limb unto that,
And the sugar-plums tumble, of
    course, to the ground –
        Hurrah for the chocolate cat!

There are marshmallows,
        gumdrops, and peppermint
        canes
        With stripings of scarlet or
        gold,
And you carry away of the treasure
    that rains
        As much as your apron can
        hold!
So come, little child, cuddle closer
    to me
        In your dainty white nightcap
        and gown,
And I'll rock you away to that
    Sugar-Plum Tree
        In the garden of Shut-Eye
        Town.

Eugene Field

29th

Fred in Bed

Go to bed, Fred,
you've had a hard day,
biting Nero,
nibbling grass
and flicking flies away.

Fred ignores the duvet
Tara makes from hay;
rests one back hoof,
stands on three,
prepares his getaway.

His drooping lip
is made from silk,
his ears are velveteen.
The yawn he yawns is yellow
and all his dreams are green.

Shirley McDermott

67

30th

The Cat of Cats

I am the cat of cats. I am
  The everlasting cat!
Cunning, and old, and sleek as jam,
  The everlasting cat!
I hunt the vermin in the night –
  The everlasting cat!
For I see best without the light –
  The everlasting cat!

William Brighty Rands

31st

Great Bear and Little Bear

High in the fields
of outer space
Great Bear and Little Bear
hold their place.

Silver coated
and pricked with light
round they go
in the plum-dark night.

I wonder whether
they growl a bit
when the wind has ice
in the tail of it?

Or if the travelling
swallows say:
Great Bear and Little Bear
went this way?

Jean Kenward

APRIL
1st – 30th

There was an old woman tossed up in a basket
Seventy times as high as the moon...

 1st

2nd

April Fool's Day

I Wonder Why Dad is So Thoroughly Mad

I wonder why Dad is so thoroughly
   mad,
I can't understand it at all,
unless it's the bee still afloat in
   his tea,
or his underwear, pinned to
   the wall.

Perhaps it's the dye on his favourite
   tie,
or the mousetrap that snapped in
   his shoe,
or the pipeful of gum that he found
   with his thumb,
or the toilet, sealed tightly
   with glue.

It can't be the bread crumbled up
   in his bed,
or the slugs someone left in
   the hall,
I wonder why Dad is so thoroughly
   mad,
I can't understand it at all.

Jack Prelutsky

My Bed is a Boat

My bed is like a little boat;
   Nurse helps me in when I embark;
She girds me in my sailor's coat
   and starts me in the dark.

At night, I go on board and say
   Good-night to all my friends on
     shore;
I shut my eyes and sail away
   And see and hear no more.

And sometimes things to bed I
   take,
   As prudent sailors have to do;
Perhaps a slice of wedding-cake,
   Perhaps a toy or two.

All night across the dark we steer:
   But when the day returns at last,
Safe in my room, beside the pier,
   I find my vessel fast.

Robert Louis Stevenson

3rd

The ABC

'Twas midnight in the schoolroom
And every desk was shut,
When suddenly from the alphabet
Was heard a loud "Tut-tut!"

Said A to B, "I don't like C;
His manners are a lack.
For all I ever see of C
Is a semi-circular back!"

"I disagree," said D to B,
"I've never found C so.
From where I stand, he seems to be
An uncompleted O."

C was vexed, "I'm much perplexed,
You criticise my shape.
I'm made like that, to help spell Cat
And Cow and Cool and Cape."

"He's right," said E; said F,
"Whoopee!"
Said G, "'Ip, 'ip, 'ooray!"
"You're dropping me," roared H to G,
"Don't do it please I pray!"

"Out of my way," L said to K.
"I'll make poor I look ILL."
To stop this stunt, J stood in front,
And presto! ILL was JILL.

"U know," said V, "that W
Is twice the age of me,
For as a Roman V is five
I'm half as young as he."

X and Y yawned sleepily,
"Look at the time!" they said.
They all jumped in to beddy byes
And the last one in was Z.

Spike Milligan

4th

The Star

Twinkle, twinkle, little star,
How I wonder what you are!
Up above the world so high,
Like a diamond in the sky.

When the blazing sun is gone,
When he nothing shines upon,
Then you show your little light,
Twinkle, twinkle, all the night.

Still your bright and tiny spark
Lights the traveller in the dark –
Though I know not what you are,
Twinkle, twinkle, little star.

Jane Taylor

5th

The Long Horse

Old horse, iron horse,
when we've all gone home,
what do you do
in the empty playpark
all alone?

Do you sleep, or dream
or just sit bored,
grumble and sigh?

Or do you sneak
from your rockers
to ride in the sky?

Tony Mitton

6th

There Was an Old Woman

There was an old woman tossed up
  in a basket
    Seventy times as high as the
      moon;
And where she was going, I couldn't
  but ask it,
    For in her hand she carried a
      broom.
"Old woman, old woman, old
  woman," quoth I,
    "Oh whither, oh whither, oh
      whither so high?"
"To sweep the cobwebs off the sky!"
  "Shall I go with you?" "Aye, by
    and by."

Anon

7th

I've Slept Everywhere

I've slept everywhere, man
I've slept everywhere
In tents and caravans, man
On beaches and in Cannes, man
In boats and trains and planes, man
In ditches, ducts and drains
I've slept everywhere

In churches and cathedrals
On hay-racks and in stables
In cafés, shops and offices
In mansions and in cottages

I've slept everywhere, man
In doorways, beside motorways
In sky-scrapers and sub-ways
On top of compost heaps, man
And underneath them streets, man
I've slept everywhere, man
Yes, I've slept everywhere!

Ivan Jones

8th

Buddha's Birthday

The Laughing Buddha

Fat monk,
sack upon his ample back
filled with sweets
and other treats
for the children of the streets
who allowed him to join in
their happy games.

The Laughing Buddha
was the fat monk's name
and how he loved to laugh,
and laugh and laugh
until his laughter
filled up every inch of space
with happiness
and simple grace.

Then, at night,
when the children had gone
and everything was done
and said,
the emptied sack became
the Laughing Buddha's bed.

Jim Hatfield

9th

The Horseman

I heard a horseman
Ride over the hill;
The moon shone clear,
The night was still;
His helm was silver,
And pale was he,
And the horse he rode
Was of ivory.

Walter de la Mare

10th

Seder Night

– Best bit, says Millie
The white, white tablecloth.
– The tablecloth! The tablecloth?
– Patterns when the light flickers,
says Millie.

– Best bit, says Sammy, the salt-
water soup,
Hard-boiled eggs all a-bobble in it.
– The salt-water soup, ach! The
salt-water soup, ach!
– But I like it, says Sammy.

– Best bit, says Sarah,
The sweet herbs, the sweet herbs,
Honey and nosh, honey and nosh.
– But not much of it, just a
   saucerful.
– I lick my finger, laughs Sarah.

– You kids, says Morry,
(Nearly barmitsvahed).
It's Pesach, Pesach.
The Four Questions are the best
   bit.

– We don't know what they mean,
   says Millie.
– Sound nice, though, says Sammy.
– Shows one kid can say Hebrew,
   says Sarah.
– It's Pesach, it's serious, says
   Morry.
You kids think it's just a party.
– It is, it is. It is a party.

And the white tablecloth floats
   on to the table
And salt-water soup, sweet herbs
And all the rest of Pesach spreads
And Solly asks The Four Questions.

– The best bit is the white, white
   tablecloth, says Millie
In the flickering candlelight.

Harold Rosen

*Seder night is the first night of Passover
which Jewish people observe by having a
special evening meal which includes some
rather interesting food*

11th

Momma's Little Baby

Momma's little baby loves
   shortenin', shortenin',
Momma's little baby loves
   shortenin' bread.
I took her to the doctor, the doctor
   said,
Momma's little baby loves
   shortenin' bread.

Put on the skillet, put on the pan,
Momma's going to make a little
   shortenin' man.
That ain't all she's gonna do,
Momma's gonna make a little
   coffee too.

Traditional American

12th

Our Cat at Night

Where does our cat go when it is
   night?
He creeps out of the house and is
   soon out of sight.
Does he roam the dark alleys or
   climb on a roof?
When he comes back in the
   morning he is quietly aloof
And treasures his secrets. He's not
   telling at all
Where he goes once he's over the
   old garden wall.

John Cotton

13th

Morningtown Ride

Train whistle blowin',
Makes a sleepy noise;
Underneath their blankets
Go all the girls and boys.

Rockin', rollin', ridin',
Out along the bay,
All bound for Morningtown,
Many miles away.

Driver at the engine,
Fireman rings the bell;
Sandman swings the lantern
To say that all is well.

Maybe it is raining
Where our train will ride;
All the little travellers
Are warm and snug inside.

Somewhere there is sunshine,
Somewhere there is day;
Somewhere there is Morningtown,
Many miles away.

Rockin', rollin', ridin',
Out along the bay,
All bound for Morningtown,
Many miles away.

Malvina Reynolds

14th

Over de Moon

Dere's a man on de moon
He's skippin an stuff,
Dere's a man on de moon
He looks very tuff,
Dere's a man on de moon
An he's all alone,
Dere's a man on de moon
His wife is at home.

He's dancing around
To real moony music,
He carries his air
He knows how to use it,
He waves to his wife
Still on Planet E,
She's waving back
But he cannot see.

De man on de moon is so clever,
He has sum ideas to pursue,
His chewing gum can last fe ever
His fast food is already chewed.

Dere's a man on de moon
He has a spaceship,
Dere's a man on de moon
An we payed fe it,
Dere's a man on de moon
His mission ain't done,
Dere's a man on de moon
He's after de Sun.

Benjamin Zephaniah

Easter Eggs

Three chocolate eggs for Easter
Left lying on my bed.
"You've had enough for one day!"
That's what Mum and Granny said.
I brushed my teeth
And washed my face –
It was time I slept,
But surely I had a little space
    For one more egg?

The first egg was tiny,
Oval-shaped and white,
Sitting on an egg-cup –
    I ate it in one bite!

The second egg was bigger,
I could hear something inside,
It rattled when I shook it –
    Oh, what did it hide?

I just had to eat it
To find the secret treasure –
A bag of chocolate buttons –
    Two sweet minutes' pleasure!

I looked at my last egg,
Tied round with a red ribbon,
Wrapped in shiny paper –
    And big as a melon!

It seemed a bit lonely
So I ate it; it was yummy!
"Leave those Easter Eggs alone!
    Bed now," called Mummy.

I brushed my teeth
And washed my face again
Now all that's left
Is silver paper and a pain
    In my tummy!

Mal Lewis Jones

16th

Now the Day is Over

Now the day is over,
  Night is drawing nigh,
Shadows of the evening
  Steal across the sky.

Now the darkness gathers,
  Stars begin to peep,
Birds and beasts and flowers
  Soon will be asleep.

Sabine Baring-Gould

17th

Aztec Song

we only came to sleep
we only came to dream
it is not true
no it is not true
that we came to live on the earth

we are changed into the grass of
    springtime
our hearts will grow green again
and they will open their petals
but our body is like a rose tree
  it puts forth flowers and then
    withers

Nahuatl Indians, Mexico
Translated by Lowell Dunham

 18th

Boring Old Bed

Here am I, in boring old bed,
My dinosaur pillowcase under my
  head.
I wish I was downstairs instead.

Mum is performing circus tricks,
Daring trapeze swinging and
  acrobat flicks,
Bareback riding with giant high
  kicks.

And here am I, in boring old bed,
My dinosaur pillowcase under my
  head.
I wish I was downstairs instead.

Dad's scuba diving in the pond,
Rescuing a mermaid, silvery and
  blonde,
Wrestling giant squid from beyond.

And here am I, in boring old bed,
My dinosaur pillowcase under my
  head.
I wish I was downstairs instead.

Even the baby is wide awake.
They've taken her down to eat jelly
  and cake.
That sleeping act is all a fake!

And here am I, in boring old bed,
My dinosaur pillowcase under my
  head.
I *am* going downstairs instead
... just to check.

Anne Adeney

19th

Snores

There's the cheeky snore, an' the
   squeaky snore,
     an' the snore that sounds like
     silk;
There's the creamy, dreamy kind of
   snore
     that comes of drinkin' milk
There's the raspy snore, an' the
   gaspy snore,
     an' the snore that's 'ard to
     wake,
An' the snore that's 'arf a jackass
   larf
     an' the hiss of a startled snake.
There's the snore that shows its
   owner's shick,
     an' the one that shows 'e's not,
And one 'oose owner I'd like to
   kick,
     the worst of all the lot.
It's a kind of cross between a calf
     an' a pig that's dyin' 'ard
With a bit thrown in from the
   mornin' din
     out in the poultry yard!

E.G. Murphy

20th

April Rain Song

Let the rain kiss you.
Let the rain beat upon your head
   with silver liquid drops.
Let the rain sing you a lullaby.

The rain makes still pools on the
   sidewalk.
The rain makes running pools in
   the gutter.
The rain plays a little sleep-song
   on our roof at night –

And I love the rain.

Langston Hughes

21st

Midnight's Moon

By midnight's moon
a river ran rune
and a blue-white swan was gliding.
And the silver leaves of a golden
    tree
shook as the stars went riding.

John Rice

22nd

Bedtime Riddle

Familiar as the light-shade on your
    lamp,
I stand firm-footed by your side all
    night
Measuring the march of minutes.

Two hands to wipe my face; no nose
    to blow,
No teeth to clean, no hair to brush
    and comb.
No ears, no eyes, no throat. And yet

My voice at dawn blares like a
    bugle call:
I bully you from bed, with my shrill
    shriek
I drag you from your dreams.

But in the dark, my whispering
    softly soothes:
A memory's echo of a cradle
    rocking:
Creak-crack ... crick-crock ...
    Tick-tock ... rock-rock...

Answer: an alarm clock

Mick Gowar

23rd

St George's Day

Dragonbirth

In the midnight mists
of long ago
on a far-off mountainside
there stood
a wild oak wood...

In the wild, wet wood
there grew an oak;
beneath the oak
there slept a cave
and in that cave
the mosses crept.

Beneath the moss
there lay a stone,
beneath the stone
there lay an egg,
and in that egg
there was a crack.

From that crack
there breathed a flame;
from that flame
there burst a fire,
and from that fire
dragon came.

Judith Nicholls

24th

You Spotted Snakes

You spotted snakes with double
  tongue,
   Thorny hedgehogs, be not seen;
Newts and blind-worms, do no
  wrong;
   Come not near our fairy queen.
    Philomel, with melody,
    Sing in our sweet lullaby;
Lulla, lulla, lullaby; lulla, lulla, lullaby!
   Never harm,
   Nor spell nor charm,
Come our lovely lady nigh;
So, good night, with lullaby.

Weaving spiders, come not here;
   Hence, you long legg'd spinners,
    hence!
Beetles black, approach not near;
   Worm nor snail, do no offence.
    Philomel, with melody,
    Sing in our sweet lullaby;
Lulla, lulla, lullaby; lulla, lulla, lullaby!
   Never harm,
   Nor spell nor charm,
Come our lovely lady nigh;
So, good night, with lullaby!

William Shakespeare (from A
Midsummer Night's Dream)

 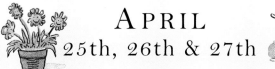

25th

The Old Wives

Two old wives sat a-talking,
A-talking, a-talking, a-talking;
Two old wives sat a-talking
About the wind and the weather –
Till their two old heads fell
  a-nodding,
A-nodding, a-nodding, a-nodding,
Till their two old heads fell
  a-nodding,
Their two old heads together.

Anon

26th

Night Fun

I hear eating.
I hear drinking.
I hear music.
I hear laughter.
Fun is something
Grown-ups never have
Before my bedtime.
Only after.

Judith Viorst

27th

Once There Was a Unicorn

Once there was a unicorn
and on the unicorn
there was a horn
(of course)
and behind the horn
there was a girl
laughing and riding,
laughing and riding,
and on the girl's head
there was hair
like the waves of the sea
dancing,
dancing,
dancing.
And she fell
slowly
silently
asleep.

Fred Sedgwick

28th

29th

The Plug-Hole Man

I know you're down there,
　Plug-hole Man,
　In the dark so utter,
For when I let the water out
　I hear you gasp and splutter.

And though I peer and peek
　and pry
　I've never seen you yet:
(I know you're down there,
　Plug-hole Man,
　In your home so wet).

But you will not be there for long
　For I've a *plan*, you see;
I'm going to catch you,
　Plug-hole Man,
　And Christian's helping me.

We'll fill the bath with water hot,
　Then give the plug a heave,
And rush down to the outside
　drain –
　And *catch* you as you leave!

Carey Blyton

Tom Scare-No-Crow

Tom Scare-crow stood in the corn
　field
to scare the farmer's crows;
he'd an old felt hat upon his head
and a bunched-up sock for a nose;
His eyes were sad and his mouth
　turned down
and he cried to himself in the rain
for he was a scare-crow who loved
　the birds
and he hated his stupid name.

One day the farmer took him down
from his bean-pole prop in the
　ground;
he carried him to the hedgerow
and there he flung Tom down.
"You're worse than useless," the
　farmer said,
"You couldn't scare crows if you
　tried –
you can lie in the hedge till you rot
　away."
"Hurrah," the scare-crow replied.

The first to arrive were the
    sparrows
with their cheeky chatter and
    cheep.
"We'll make our nest in his pocket,
    it's warm and dark and deep."
"There's room for me," piped the
    robin,
"In the top of his Wellington boot."
"I can perch on his old felt hat,"
he heard the owl hoot.

Now if you pass that hedgerow
when the world is fast asleep
you may hear the owl hooting
and baby birds sleepily cheep.
There's a smile on the face of the
    Scare-no-crow
and his dreams are happy
    and bright
for his straw-filled heart is full
    of love
as he sleeps in the pale moonlight.

Pamela G. Hodge

Tom made himself comfy in the
    ditch
on a cushion of moss and leaves;
he undid his old tweed jacket
and pulled the stick from his
    sleeves;
He pushed his hat to the back of
    his head
and his mouth turned up in a smile,
"I know they'll come," the scare-
    crow said,
"If I wait a little while."

30th

Escape at Bedtime

The lights from the parlour and
  kitchen shone out
  Through the blinds and the
    windows and bars;
And high overhead and all moving
  about,
  There were thousands of millions
    of stars.
There ne'er were such thousands of
  leaves on a tree,
  Nor of people in church or the
    Park,
As the crowds of the stars that
  looked down upon me,
  And that glittered and winked in
    the dark.

The Dog, and the Plough, and the
  Hunter, and all,
  And the star of the sailor, and
    Mars,
These shone in the sky, and the pail
  by the wall
  Would be half full of water and
    stars.
They saw me at last, and they
  chased me with cries,
  And they soon had me packed into
    bed;
But the glory kept shining and
  bright in my eyes,
  And the stars going round in my
    head.

Robert Louis Stevenson

MAY
1st – 31st

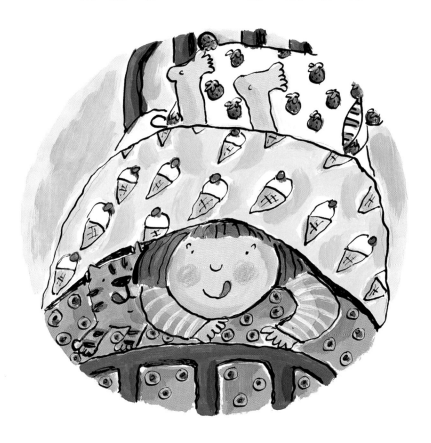

*Strawberry pillows, ice-cream sheets,
  sugar-coated blankets sprinkled with sweets...*

2nd

1st

May Day

The Maypole

Alone on the green the Maypole
  stands,
    its ribbons dangling down,
No longer the hub of the dancing
  girls
    weaving their patterns around.

Alone on the green the Maypole
  stands,
    tall and straight and proud
Though the music and laughter
  have died away
    and nothing is left of the crowd.

Alone on the green the Maypole
  stands,
    Queen of the May for tonight
The moon has clothed it in silver
  strands
    and crowned it with golden
      light.

Mal Lewis Jones

Ten in the Bed

There were ten in the bed and the
  little one said,
Roll over, roll over,
So they all rolled over and one
  fell out.
He hit the floor and gave a shout!

*Please remember to tie a knot in
  your pyjamas –
Single beds are only made for one!*

They kept on rolling and two
  fell out.
Two hit the floor and gave a shout!

They kept on rolling and three
  fell out.
Three hit the floor and gave a
  shout!

They kept on rolling and four
  fell out.
Four hit the floor and gave a shout!

There were none in the bed and the
  little one said,
Good night!

Anon

3rd

God

The moon is a silver hubcap
up in the sky.
It is on God's unicycle.
He rides up high.

On the motorway in the black sky
the stars are streetlights
for God
to show him where to fly.

The planets are traffic lights.
Mars is a red stoplight.
At Saturn he has to wait.
When he gets to Jupiter
he has to go.

The clouds are God's thought
  balloons
sailing by.
He thinks about what we're doing.
He knows I am writing a poem
  now.

Laura Ranger (6)

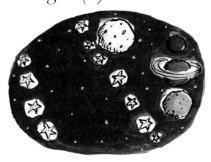

4th

Sitting in My Bathtub

Sitting in my bathtub,
I have sailed the seven seas.
I have anchored by the taps.
I've been shipwrecked off the knees.

I have sailed into the unknown
To beat off an attack
From a fleet of pirates lurking
Round behind my back.

I have sailed between the fingers
Where no other ship has been.
I've explored the murky depths
In a soapy submarine.

Sitting in my bathtub,
I have sailed the seven seas.
I have anchored by the taps.
I've been shipwrecked off the knees.

John Foster

5th

Old Shellover

"Come!" said old Shellover.
"What?" says Creep.
"The horny old Gardener's fast
    asleep;
The fat cock Thrush
To his nest has gone;
And the dew shines bright
In the rising moon;
Old Sallie Worm from her hole
    doth peep:
"Come!" said Old Shellover.
"Ay!" said Creep.

Walter de la Mare

6th

The Sea in the Trees

When the warm wind was flowing
In the leaves of the tall ash tree,
The old man fell asleep in the park
And he dreamed the sound of the
    the sea.

The branches filled and billowed,
The high mainmast swayed,
As long sea-miles of the afternoon
His green galleon made.

In the harbour of the shade.

Kit Wright

7th

8th

Noises in the Night

Midnight's bell goes ting, ting, ting,
 ting, ting,
Then dogs do howl, and not a bird
 does sing
But the nightingale, and she goes
 twit, twit, twit.
Owls then on every bough do sit,
Ravens croak on chimney tops,
The cricket in the chamber hops,
And the cats cry mew, mew, mew.
The nibbling mouse is not asleep,
But he goes peep, peep, peep, peep.
 And the cats cry mew, mew,
  mew,
 And still the cats cry mew, mew,
  mew.

Thomas Middleton

Bedtime, Rhymetime

It's bedtime, it's rhymetime,
it's churchbells cease their chime
 time.

It's bedtime, it's teddytime,
it's pyjamas at the readytime.

It's bedtime, it's tunetime,
it's watch the milky moontime.

It's bedtime, it's blisstime,
it's one more goodnight kisstime.

John Rice

Not a Bit Sleepy

I know I'm in bed,
But I really must say
I'm not a bit sleepy
And wish you would stay.

You could read me a story
A poem or two.
And then we'll consider
The next thing to do.

That reading you've started
Is one of the best.
I'll just snuggle down
To hear all the rest.

I'm still wide awake,
And shall be for ages;
So you *could* carry on
For pages and pages.

Word follows word, and it's
Something I've found,
As well as their meaning,
I do love their sound.

If my eyelids should close
For a second or so,
It means I can listen
Much better, you know.

But now you seem fainter
And further away.
You speak, but I hardly
Can hear what you say.

It's all very soothing,
And so, I suppose,
That just for a moment
I might have a dozzzzzzze.

Barry On

10th

I Asked the Little Boy Who Cannot See

I asked the little boy who cannot
   see,
"And what is colour like?"
"Why, green," said he,
"Is like the rustle when the wind
   blows through
The forest; running water, that
   is blue;
And red is like a trumpet sound;
   and pink
Is like the smell of roses; and
   I think
That purple must be like a thunder
   storm;
And yellow is like something soft
   and warm;
And white is a pleasant stillness
   when you lie
And dream."

Anon

11th

Spider

I'm told that the spider
Has coiled up inside her
Enough silky material
To spin an aerial
One-way track
To the moon and back;
Whilst I
cannot even catch a fly.

Frank Collymore

95

12th

Bats

A bat is born
Naked and blind and pale.
His mother makes a pocket of her
   tail
And catches him. He clings to her
   long fur
By his thumbs and toes and teeth.
And then the mother dances
   through the night
Doubling and looping, soaring,
   somersaulting –
Her baby hangs on underneath.
All night, in happiness, she hunts
   and flies.
Her high sharp cries
Like shining needlepoints of sound
Go out into the night and, echoing
   back,
Tell her what they have touched.
She hears how far it is, how big
   it is,
Which way it's going:
She lives by hearing.
The mother eats the moths and
   gnats she catches
In full flight; in full flight
The mother drinks the water of the
   pond

She skims across. Her baby hangs
on tight.
Her baby drinks the milk she
   makes him
In moonlight or starlight, in
   mid-air.
Their single shadow, printed on
   the moon
Or fluttering across the stars,
Whirls on all night; at daybreak
The tired mother flaps home to her
   rafter.
The others all are there.
They hang themselves up by their
   toes,
They wrap themselves in their
   brown wings.
Bunched upside down, they sleep
   in air.
Their sharp ears, their sharp teeth,
   their quick sharp faces
Are dull and slow and mild.
All the bright day, as the mother
   sleeps,
She folds her wings about her
   sleeping child.

Randall Jarrell

Hush Little Baby

Hush little baby, don't say a word,
Momma's gonna buy you a
  mocking-bird.

If that mocking-bird won't sing,
Momma's gonna buy you a
  diamond ring.

If that diamond ring turns to brass,
Momma's gonna buy you a
  looking-glass.

If that looking-glass gets broke,
Momma's gonna buy you a
  billy-goat.

If that billy-goat won't pull,
Momma's gonna buy you a cart
  and bull.

If that cart and bull turn over,
Momma's gonna buy you a dog
  named Rover.

If that dog named Rover runs away,
Momma's gonna buy you another
  some day.

Hush little baby, don't say a word,
Momma's gonna buy you a
  mocking-bird.

Traditional American

14th

15th

Strawberry Pillows, Ice-Cream Sheets

Storms

The night I got sent to bed
   without any tea,
The moment I lay down my head
   what did I see?

Strawberry pillows,
   ice-cream sheets,
sugar-coated blankets
   sprinkled with sweets,
chocolate buttons on
   sponge pyjamas,
marshmallow mattress with
   honey-soaked bananas.

My mouth began to water
   at the thought of such a treat,
But suddenly I woke up –

   my mouth crammed full of
   SHEET!

Ivan Jones

We tiptoe across the
carpet sea to bed,
and never tread
on the Lego bricks,
like Grandpa does.

We know just where
our toes can go,
between the pens
and the railway line,
around the garage,
and never tread
on the cars,
like Grandma does.

The bed is a pirate ship
in a dark, dark storm,
and the waves have
tossed the toys across
the floor.

So we always swim,
over the mess, to the door,
and turn on the light,
before Grandpa and
Grandma come
to say goodnight.

Maggie Simmans

16th

A Dream

I dreamed a dream next Tuesday
    week,
      Beneath the apple-trees;
I thought my eyes were big pork-
    pies,
      And my nose was Stilton
      cheese.
The clock struck twenty minutes
    to six,
      When a frog sat on my knee;
I asked him to lend me eighteen
    pence
      But he borrowed a shilling of
      me.

Anon

17th

from The Night-Piece, to Julia

Her eyes the glow-worm lend thee,
The shooting stars attend thee;
    And the elves also,
    Whose little eyes glow,
Like the sparks of fire, befriend
    thee.

No will-o'-th'-wisp mis-light thee,
Nor snake, or slow-worm bite thee:
    But on, on thy way
    Not making a stay,
Since ghost there's none to affright
    thee.

Let not the dark thee cumber:
What though the moon does
    slumber?
    The stars of the night
    Will lend thee their light,
Like tapers clear without number.

Robert Herrick

 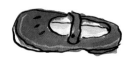
18th

The Dustman

When the shades of night are
  falling, and the sun goes down,
O! the Dustman comes a-creeping
  in from Shut-eye Town.
And he throws dust in the eyes of
  all the babies that he meets,
No matter where he finds them,
  in the house, or in the streets.
Then the babies' eyes grow heavy
  and the lids drop down,
When the Dustman comes
  a-creeping in from Shut-eye Town.

When mother lights the lamps and
  draws the curtains down,
O! the Dustman comes a-creeping
  in from Shut-eye Town,
For he shuts their eyes at nightfall,
  just when they want to see.
But their little limbs are weary, for
  all they fret and frown,
When the Dustman comes
  a-creeping in from Shut-eye Town.

Anon

19th

Ariel's Song

Where the bee sucks, there suck I:
In a cowslip's bell I lie;
There I couch when owls do cry.
On the bat's back I do fly
After summer merrily:
Merrily, merrily shall I live now
Under the blossom that hangs on
  the bough.

*William Shakespeare
(from The Tempest)*

100

Ten Tired Tigers

Ten tired tigers asleep in Tiger
    Bay
Nine tired nanny-goats napping on
    the hay
Eight tired elephants dozing by a
    tree
Seven tired sea-lions floating on
    the sea
Six tired skunks snoring on their
    own
Five tired frogs stretched out on a
    stone
Four tired flamingoes resting on
    one leg
Three tired thrushes sitting on
    their eggs
Two tired tortoises sleeping in a
    shed
One tired Teddy tucked up in my
    bed

Ivan Jones

21st

Old Songs

Old songs do not die
they drift on up
they linger high
into the atmosphere
where
they whisper into lonely ear.
Old songs are always there,
they strain right up
towards the moon
then tinkle down
upon new tunes.

Pauline Stewart

22nd

Good Night Moon

"The clouds make a pillow
for my big, bright head.

The stars are the pattern
on my blue bed-spread.

I'm sleepy and I'm stretchy
so I'm going off to bed."

That's what the moon,
with a big yawn, said.

Tony Mitton

23rd

Morning Prayer

Now another day is breaking,
Sleep was sweet and so is waking,
Dear Lord, I promised you last
   night
Never again to sulk or fight.
Such vows are easier to keep
When a child is sound asleep.
Today, O Lord, for your dear sake,
I'll try to keep them when awake.

Ogden Nash

24th

The Owl and the Pussy-cat

The Owl and the Pussy-cat went
  to sea
 In a beautiful pea-green boat;
They took some honey, and plenty
  of money
 Wrapped up in a five-pound note.
The Owl looked up to the stars
  above,
 And sang to a small guitar,
"O lovely Pussy, O Pussy, my love,
 What a beautiful Pussy you are,
    You are, you are!
What a beautiful Pussy you are!"

Pussy said to the Owl, "You
  elegant fowl,
 How charmingly sweet you sing!
Oh! let us be married; too long we
  have tarried:
 But what shall we do for a ring?"
They sailed away, for a year and a
  day,
 To the land where the bong-tree
  grows;
And there in a wood a Piggy-wig
  stood,
 With a ring at the end of his nose,
    His nose, his nose,
With a ring at the end of his nose.

"Dear Pig, are you willing to sell
  for one shilling
 Your ring?" Said the Piggy, "I
  will."
So they took it away, and were
  married next day
 By the turkey who lives on the
  hill.
They dined on mince and slices of
  quince,
 Which they ate with a runcible
  spoon;
And hand in hand, on the edge of
  the sand,
 They danced by the light of the
  moon,
    The moon, the moon,
They danced by the light of the
  moon.

Edward Lear

25th

White Dog, Black Beach

White dog,
Black beach.
Green sea,
Out of reach.
Blue sky,
Black cliff.
Purple heather,
Shakes and dips.
Grass green,
Slate grey.
Silver pools,
Golden day.
Orange bucket,
Pink spade.
Wooden boat,
Home-made.
Silver fish
Caught by me.
My new shoes
Drift out to sea.

Trouble waits,
Sharp as a smack.
Charlie swims
To get them back.
Emerald ocean
At his throat.
White spray,
Passing boat.
Back on shore,
Umber weeds,
Golden crabs,
Dancing reeds.
Golden reeds,
Sinking sun.
Home to bed,
Everyone.

Pauline Fisk

104

26th

The White Seal's Lullaby

Oh! hush thee, my baby, the night
  is behind us,
    And black are the waters that
      sparkled so green.
The moon, o'er the combers, looks
  downward to find us
    At rest in the hollows that
      rustle beween.

Where billow meets billow, there
  soft be thy pillow;
    Ah, weary wee flipperling, curl at
      thy ease!
The storm shall not wake thee, nor
  shark overtake thee,
    Asleep in the arms of the slow-
      swinging seas.

Rudyard Kipling

27th

The Kangaroo

Water beneath the hills,
running slowly from the creek,
towards the hills.

Birds sitting on the branch,
smelling the red flowers
that are growing.

Kangaroo is lying in the shade,
very tired from hopping around,
he listens to the water,
that is running very slowly.

He is happy, no people around,
to spear him.
He smells the red flowers,
so tired he goes to sleep.

Pansy Rose Napaljarri

 28th

The Bestest Bear Song

Oh,
this is the bear,
the very best bear,
the best *bestest* best bear
of all.
But it's lost one leg,
and it's lost one eye,
and it's spotty,
and it's grotty
and it's small.
But
this is the bear,
the very best bear,
the best *bestest* best bear
of all.
    YES SIR!

It's wobbly and worn,
and its left ear is torn
yet it's been with me
since the day I was born,
and I love,
oh, I love its soft fur.
For
this is the bear,
the very best bear,
the best *bestest* best bear
of all.
    YES SIR!

Wes Magee

29th

30th

The Moon

The moon is a banana shape
That hangs
Up in the sky.
And when the sun
Has turned away,
The moon is there
To take its place,
To shine down on the earth
With a smiling face.
Its moonbeams are a slide
Where the fairies play.

Jamie Booth (6)

My Moccasins Have Not Walked

My moccasins have not walked
Among the giant forest trees

My leggings have not brushed
Against the fern and berry bush

My medicine pouch has not been
    filled
With roots and herbs and sweet-
    grass

My hands have not fondled the
    spotted fawn

My eyes have not beheld
The golden rainbow of the north

My hair has not been adorned
With the eagle feather

Yet
My dreams are dreams of these
My heart is one with them
The scent of them caresses my soul

Duke Redbird

31st

A Song at Bedtime

Haven't I had
A busy day!
More than Mum or Dad
I'd say.

From top to toe
And back to top
I've been on the go
Without a stop.

I haven't missed
A single minute,
Time can't resist
When I begin it.

How it's passed!
I've watched TV,
I've eaten breakfast,
Lunch and tea,

I've whispered, shouted,
Rushed around,
I've inned and outed,
Up and down.

Oh, what a pace!
I'm out of breath!
I've washed my face,
I've cleaned my teeth,

I've said goodnight
To everyone,
I'm tucked up tight
But not *quite* done.

There's one thing more
Before I go,
I'm ready for
My poem now!

John Mole

JUNE
1st – 30th

There was a man lived in the moon

And his name was Aiken Drum...

1st

Dog

Asleep he wheezes at his ease.
He only wakes to scratch his fleas.

He hogs the fire, he bakes his head
As if it were a loaf of bread.

He's just a sack of snoring dog.
You can lug him like a log.

You can roll him with your foot.
He'll stay snoring where he's put.

Take him out for exercise
He'll roll in cowclap up to his eyes.

He will not race, he will not romp.
He saves his strength for gobble
   and chomp.

He'll work as hard as you could
   wish
Emptying the dinner dish.

Then flops flat, and digs down
   deep,
Like a miner, into sleep.

Ted Hughes

2nd

My Crocodile

My crocodile is very small.
He has no claws or teeth at all.
He doesn't scratch.
He doesn't bite.
He's safe to take to bed at night.

I love his little beady eyes.
I love him more than lullabies.
I love his cheeky crockish grin.
So don't forget to tuck him in.

For when he's there, I'm glad to
   say,
He helps to snap bad dreams away.

Tony Mitton

3rd

Aiken Drum

There was a man lived in the
  moon,
Lived in the moon, lived in the
  moon,
There was a man lived in the
  moon,
And his name was Aiken Drum.

And he played upon a ladle,
A ladle, a ladle,
And he played upon a ladle,
And his name was Aiken Drum.

And his hat was made of good
  cream cheese,
Good cream cheese, good cream
  cheese,
And his hat was made of good
  cream cheese,
And his name was Aiken drum.

And his coat was made of good
  roast beef,
Good roast beef, good roast beef,
And his coat was made of good
  roast beef,
And his name was Aiken Drum.

And his buttons were made of
  penny loaves,
Penny loaves, penny loaves,
And his buttons were made of
  penny loaves,
And his name was Aiken Drum.

His waistcoat was made of crust of
  pies,
Crust of pies, crust of pies,
His waistcoat was made of crust of
  pies,
And his name was Aiken Drum.

His trousers were made of haggis
  bags,
Haggis bags, haggis bags,
His trousers were made of haggis
  bags
And his name was Aiken drum.

And he played upon a ladle,
A ladle, a ladle,
And he played upon a ladle,
And his name was Aiken Drum.

Anon

111

4th

Night-Light

Night-light,
Night-light,
What do you see?
I see you –
Can you see me?

I see a sleepy ceiling,
I see a sleepy floor,
I see soft, sleepy curtains,
I see a sleepy door.

I see a sleepy toy chest,
I see a silent ball,
I see a sleepy picture
Nodding on the wall.

I see a sleepy window,
I see a sleepy chair,
I see a sleepy, sleepy blanket
And a yawning teddy bear.

Night-light,
Night-light,
What do you see?
I see you –
Can you see me?

Eve Merriam

5th

Bedbugs Marching Song

Bedbugs
Have the right
To bite.

Bedbugs
Of the world
Unite.

Don't let
These humans
Sleep too tight.

John Agard

6th

The Rock-a-By Lady

The Rock-a-By Lady from Hushaby
    Street
        Comes stealing; comes creeping;
The poppies they hang from her
    head to her feet,
And each hath a dream that is tiny
    and fleet –
She bringeth her poppies to you, my
    sweet,
        When she findeth you sleeping!

There is one little dream of a
    beautiful drum –
        "Rub-a-dub!" it goeth;
There is one little dream of a big
    sugar-plum,
And lo! thick and fast the other
    dreams come
Of popguns that bang, and tin tops
    that hum,
        And a trumpet that bloweth!

And dollies peep out of those wee
    little dreams
        With laughter and singing;
And boats go a-floating on silvery
    streams,
And the stars peek-a-boo with their
    own misty gleams,

And up, up and up, where Mother
    Moon beams,
        The fairies go winging!

Would you dream all these dreams
    that are tiny and fleet?
        They'll come to you sleeping;
So shut the two eyes that are weary,
    my sweet,
For the Rock-a-By Lady from
    Hushaby Street
With poppies that hang from her
    head to her feet,
        Comes stealing; comes creeping.

Eugene Field

113

7th

8th

With a Grandchild

Bed in Summer

We walked around the sea, that
  evening on the island,
Not round the island, look you! but
  we walked around the sea.
And I was old and frosted, while
  you were less than seven,
But my heart came leaping
  laughing from the place it used
  to be.
And all the winds of heaven from
  the sea around the island
Brought messages from continents
  and countries severally.
Blue breezes from Antarctica,
  warm apple breath from Devon,
Spices from Samarkand astride the
  little clouds of heaven,
An old tang of the tundra, and the
  sulphur-steaming crater,
The fragrant sea-filled night of
  hanging stars on the Equator,
The crushed grape from the vine-
  yards with the orange trees of
   Spain,
The sodden sob and heartbreak of
  England in the rain...
And you lent me sixty summers...
  but I gave them back again.

Ursula Moray Williams

In winter I get up at night
And dress by yellow candle-light.
In summer, quite the other way,
I have to go to bed by day.

I have to go to bed and see
The birds still hopping on the tree,
Or hear the grown-up people's feet
Still going past me in the street.

And does it not seem hard to you,
When all the sky is clear and blue,
And I should like so much to play,
To have to go to bed by day?

Robert Louis Stevenson

 9th

Banyan Tree

Moonshine tonight, come mek we
    dance and sing,
Moonshine tonight, come mek we
    dance and sing,
Me deh rock so, yu deh rock so,
    under banyan tree,
Me deh rock so, yu deh rock so,
    under banyan tree.

Ladies mek curtsy, an gentlemen
    mek bow,
Ladies mek curtsy, an gentlemen
    mek bow,
Me deh rock so, yu deh rock so,
    under banyan tree,
Me deh rock so, yu deh rock so,
    under banyan tree.
Den we join hans an dance around
    an roun,
Den we join hans an dance around
    an roun,
Me deh rock so, yu deh rock so,
    under banyan tree,
Me deh rock so, yu deh rock so,
    under banyan tree.

Traditional Jamaican

 10th

Girls and Boys
Come Out to Play

Girls and boys come out to play,
The moon doth shine as bright as
    day.
Leave your supper and leave your
    sleep
And come with your playfellows in
    the street.
Come with a whoop, come with a
    call,
Come with a good will, or come
    not at all.
Up the ladder and down the wall,
A halfpenny roll will serve us all.
You find milk, and I'll find flour,
And we'll have pudding in half an
    hour.

Anon

The Big Rock Candy Mountains

One evenin' as the sun went down
And the jungle fire was burnin',
Down the track came a hobo hikin',
And he said: Boys, I'm not turnin',
I'm headed for a land that's far
    away
Beside the crystal fountains,
So come with me, we'll all go see
The Big Rock Candy Mountains.

> *O ... the ... buzzin' of the bees*
> *In the cigarette trees,*
> *The sodawater fountains,*
> *Near the lemonade springs,*
> *Where the bluebird sings*
> *In the Big Rock Candy Mountains.*

In the Big Rock Candy Mountains,
There's a land that's fair and
    bright,
Where the money grows on bushes,
And you sleep out every night.
Where the box cars are all empty
And the sun shines every day,

O I'm bound to go, where there
    ain't no snow,
Where the rain don't fall and the
    wind don't blow,
In the Big Rock Candy Mountains.

In the Big Rock Candy Mountains,
All the cats have wooden legs,
The bulldogs all have rubber teeth,
And the hens lay soft-boiled eggs.
The farmers' trees are full of fruit,
And the barns are full of hay.
There's a lake of stew and of
    whisky too,
You can paddle all around 'em in a
    big canoe,
In the Big Rock Candy Mountains.

> *O ... the ... buzzin' of the bees*
> *In the cigarette trees,*
> *The sodawater fountains,*
> *Near the lemonade springs,*
> *Where the bluebird sings*
> *In the Big Rock Candy Mountains.*

American folk song

12th

Grey Cells

When you go to sleep
What happens to your brain?
Does it go off on its own
For a toddle down the lane?

Or does it say to itself,
I've been working hard all day,
I'll slip into something more
    comfortable
And then go out to play?

Or does it go into orbit
Like a satellite,
Spinning round and round the
    world
Until the end of night?

Whatever it does, I must admit
When I wake up each day,
I'm glad my brain is back in my
    head
Ready for the fray.

Ivan Jones

13th

Night Hunter

All must be still when the barn owl
    flies,
Whiskers and feet and tails!
Watch for the mask with the round
    black eyes
And the wings like great white
    sails.

All will be well when the barn owl
    glides
Back to his high dark den.
Wise is the vole or shrew that
    hides
When his cry is heard again!

Sue Cowling

14th

Rooming House

The blind man draws his curtains
  for the night
and goes to bed, leaving a burning
  light

above the bathroom mirror.
  Through the wall,
he hears the deaf man walking
  down the hall

in his squeaky shoes to see if
  there's a light
under the blind man's door, and all
  is right.

Ted Kooser

15th

Will There Really Be a Morning?

Will there really be a morning?
Is there such a thing as day?
Could I see it from the mountains
If I were as tall as they?

Has it feet like water lilies?
Has it feathers like a bird?
Is it brought from famous countries
Of which I have never heard?

Oh, some scholar! Oh, some sailor!
Oh, some wise man from the skies!
Please to tell a little pilgrim
Where the place called morning
  lies!

Emily Dickinson

JUNE
16th

16th

What Can Be Got Out of Bedtime?

Well, let me see;
There's BED
And TED
And TEE
And BE.

There's TIM
(He's DIM!)
And DEE
(Who's she?)

There's BIDE
And TIDE
And TIE
And DIE.

There's ITEM
And BITE 'EM.
What more can we see?
There's TIME to find MITE
And to BID for a BEE.

There's BET
And the DEBT
That then must be MET.
There's EDIT and BIT
(And that's almost IT).

That's not a bad list,
I think you'll agree;
But the best I can get
Out of BEDTIME is ME!

Barry On

17th

What's That?

What's that rustling at the
    window?
Only the curtain flapping in the
    breeze.

What's that groaning in the
    garden?
Only the branches swaying in the
    trees.

What's that rattling at the front
    door?
Only the wind in the letter-box
    flap.

What's that drumming in the
    bathroom?
Only the dripping of the leaking
    tap.

What's that hissing in the front
    room?
Only the gas as it burns in the fire.

What's that murmur in the
    kitchen?
Only the whirring of the tumble
    drier.

What's that shadow lurking
    in the corner beside the door?
It's only your clothes where you
    left them
        lying on the bedroom floor.

John Foster

The Dancing Tiger

There's a quiet, gentle tiger
In the woods below the hill,
And he dances on his tiptoes,
When the world is dreaming still.
So you only ever hear him
In the silence of the night,
And you only ever see him
When the full moon's shining
    bright.

One Summer night I saw him
    first –
Twirling, whirling round.
And when I gasped aloud in fright,
He knew that he'd been found.
He turned to me and whispered,
"Please don't tell them that I'm
    here."
The laughter in his lightning eyes
Swept away my fear.
"If you will keep me secret –
Never tell a soul –
Then you can come and dance with
    me,
On nights the moon is whole."

So once a month, from then till
    now,
I've tiptoed to the wood.
We've swirled and swayed among
    the trees,
As Tiger said we could.
We've skipped in Spring through
    bluebells,
In Summer circled slow,
We've high-kicked in the Autumn
    leaves,
And waltzed in Winter snow.

But now that I am eighty-two
My dancing nights are done.
I've chosen you, great-grandchild,
To share my dream, so come
With me into the woods of sleep –
The full moon's shining high –
I'll sit and watch you dancing both
Beneath the starbright sky.

Malachy Doyle

19th

Night in the Jungle

Night in the jungle.
Taxis prowl,
Ambulances yelp,
Late buses growl,

Aeroplanes screech,
Tugboats grunt,
Freight trains chatter,
Police cars hunt.

Metal monsters
Surround my den –
Daylight comes
And they're tame again!

Sue Cowling

20th

Midsummer's Eve

Who Believes in Fairies?

No one believes in fairies now,
tiny flittery things
with see-through wings.
No one believes they are true.
I don't. Do you?

Well – sometimes –
on summer nights
when the patio door is open
and the breeze makes strange
noises among the trees;
when the stars glitter
and silver moonshine
sparkles and flashes
between the leaves;
when our dog on the lawn
sits dead still
and stares, just stares
at thin air – well –
I do wonder.

Patricia Leighton

22nd

Hide and Seek

At night, the stars fall out of bed,
For them the dark is day instead.
The moon is bright, it's time to
    play,
Hide and seek with the Milky Way.

Andrew Fusek Peters

23rd

Charity Chadder

Charity Chadder
Borrowed a ladder,
Leaned it against the moon,
Climbed to the top
Without a stop
On the 31st of June,
Brought down every single star,
Kept them all in a pickle jar.

Charles Causley

21st

What If

What if
my bed grew wings and I could fly
    away in my bed.
I would fly to the top of a high
    block of flats,
look out over all the streets
and then come floating slowly
    down to the ground.

I would fly to a misty island near
    Japan
and watch fishing boats cross the
    sea.

If my bed grew wings I would fly
    to a thick forest
where there was an old broken-
    down castle
that no one knew about, hidden in
    the trees.
And wherever I went
and whatever I saw,
all the time I was in my bed.

Michael Rosen

24th

My Dad, Your Dad

My dad's fatter than your dad,
Yes, my dad's fatter than yours;
If he eats any more he won't fit in
    the house,
He'll have to live out of doors.

Yes, but my dad's balder than your
    dad,
My dad's balder, OK,
He's only got two hairs left on his
    head
And both are turning grey.

Ah, but my dad's thicker than your
    dad,
My dad's thicker, all right.
He has to look at his watch to see
If it's noon or the middle of the
    night.

Yes, but my dad's more boring than
    your dad.
If he ever starts counting sheep
When he can't get to sleep at
    night, he finds
It's the sheep that go to sleep.

But my dad doesn't mind your dad.
Mine quite likes yours too.
I suppose they don't always think
    much of us!
That's true, I suppose, that's true.

Kit Wright

25th

Minnie and Winnie

Minnie and Winnie
  Slept in a shell.
Sleep, little ladies!
  And they slept well.

Pink was the shell within,
  Silver without;
Sounds of the great sea
  Wandered about.

Sleep, little ladies,
  Wake not soon!
Echo on echo
  Dies to the moon.

Two bright stars
  Peeped into the shell.
"What are they dreaming of?
  Who can tell?"

Started a green linnet
  Out of the croft;
Wake, little ladies,
  The sun is aloft!

Alfred, Lord Tennyson

26th

Stargrazing

If the sun was made of birthday
    cake
    I'd eat at least six slices.
If the moon was made of
    marmalade
    ah, sweet oranges and spices.

If space was made of lemonade
    to swim would be amazing.
If stars were tiny lollipops
    I'd spend my nights stargrazing!

John Rice

27th

Bedtime Tactics

I know it sounds silly
In the summer, but I'm chilly:
    Can I have a hot-water bottle,
    Mum?

I know I ought to be asleep
And I have tried counting sheep:
    But can I have a quick drink,
    Mum?

I know I really oughtn't
But I thought it was important:
    Can I tell you something,
    Mum?

Now I've forgotten what it was,
But can I have a kiss because...
    Can I have another cuddle,
    Mum?

I know it's not a dark night,
But you forgot the landing light:
    Can you put the light on,
    Mum?

Yes, I thought I was ready,
But I'd forgotten Teddy:
    Can *he* have a little kiss, Mum?

No, it's not hot-water bottles or a
    drink or the light;
You did kiss Teddy and me all
    right;
It's just I forgot to say "Night-
    night":
    I'll be off to bed now, Mum!

Celia Warren

28th

Ducks at Dawn

"Quack! Quack!"
Said seven ducks at dawn
While night dew
Glimmered on the lawn.

"Quack! Quack!" they said.
"It's time to eat.
We'll go hunt mushrooms
For a treat."

   And in the light
   Of early dawn
   I saw them chasing
   On the lawn.

They sought their treat
With hungry quacks
And marked the dew
With criss-cross tracks.

They ate the mushrooms
One by one
And quacked to greet
The rising sun.

   But in my bed
   I settled back
   And slept to tunes
   Of "Quack! Quack! Quack!"

James S. Tippett

29th

My Book of Animals

Let's both sit here and take a look
at all the animals in my book.

See this brown bear. Bet he can
   growl.
And there's a tiger on the prowl.

I like those lions in the sun
and, oh, striped zebras on the run.

Count the elephants. One. Two.
   Three.
Ha! Silly monkeys up a tree.

Here's a camel, and here's a snake,
and there's a hippo in the lake.

It's great to sit and take a look
at all the animals in my book.

Wes Magee

30th

Jerboa

In Asia, he has five toes, in Africa
   only three,
But everywhere he has a bottle-
   brush tail, long and sinewy.
He's an Olympic jumper, this six-
   inch jerboa,
he can jump ten times his own
   height,
and when the moon shines bright
   in sandy Morocco a
party he'll hold with delight;
with the other jerboa he'll leap and
   he'll play
till he runs underground at the
   dawn of the day.

Marjorie Baker

128

JULY
1st – 31st

Old Jumpety-Bumpety-Hop-and-Go-One
Was lying asleep on his side in the sun...

1st

Mooning

What shall we do? O what can we
   do?
The Man in the Moon has lost his
   shoe –

We'll search all night on the
   rubbish-dump
For a star-spangled sneaker or a
   moon-bright pump.

What shall we do? O what can we
   do?
Now he's gone and lost his
   trousers too.

We'll search all night and hope to
   find
Something that will warm his bare
   behind.

It's a bit strange and it's a bit sad
But the Man in the Moon has gone
   quite mad.

He is flinging away all his clothes
And where they'll end up nobody
   knows.

So don't look at the sky, don't
   look, it's rude –
The Man in the Moon is completely
   nude!

Brian Patten

2nd

Five Little Owls

Five little owls in an old elm tree,
Fluffy and puffy as owls could be,
Blinking and winking with big
   round eyes
At the big round moon that hung
   in the skies:
As I passed beneath I could hear
   one say,
"There'll be mouse for supper,
   there will, today!"
Then all of them hooted, "Tu-whit,
   tu-whoo
Yes, mouse for supper, hoo hoo,
   hoo hoo!"

Anon

3rd

My Baby Sister's Room

The baby's happy, the room is
   giggling
rattling, jiggling in wide-eyed
   surprise
as everything in it is made new,
   amazing,
never been seen before

The baby's grumpy, the room aches
torn by hopeless howls, filled
with a worn-out cloud drizzling
cold rain and a smell of sick

The baby's sleeping, the room
is drowsy, purrs like a comfortable
   cat,
smells warm and milky, falls into
a dream where everyone sleepwalks
   softly.

Dave Calder

4th

Independence Day

Fourth of July

Shout hurray for the fourth of July
For that's the night the fireworks
fly!

We've already eaten hot dogs and
cake
And all the cookies our mothers
could bake.

We watched the parade march
through the town,
The band and the Mayor and Coco
the clown.

We listened to speeches – our
country's great!
Freedom for all in every state.

But now silver streaks soar through
the sky,
Explode with loud bangs, way up
high.

Blazing sparks spin from a
Catherine wheel,
Whipping round and round like a
silvery eel.

Volcanoes erupt, firecrackers whizz,
Rainbows cascade and sparklers
fizz.

It's the part of the day that I like
best,
Better than food, parades, all the
rest!

Anne Adeney

JULY
5th

5th

A Poem Just Like This

Daddy came home and he read to me,
He read to me, he read to me,
Daddy came home and he read to me
A poem *just like this!*

Daddy came home and he said to me,
In bed to me, he said to me,
Daddy came home and he said to me
A poem *just like this!*

And then he gave me a kiss.

And then he said, "Sleep tight!"

And then he put out the light.

BUT

You know, the other night...

Daddy came home and he read to me,
In bed to me, he read to me,
Daddy came home and he read to me
And I didn't make a peep.

And before he'd finished the *poem like this*

And before he gave me a goodnight kiss

And before he said, "Goodnight. Sleep tight!"

And before he got up and put out the light

Daddy was

Fast

Asleep!

Kit Wright

6th

7th

Cat in the Dark

The Kangaroo

Mother, Mother, what was that?
Hush, my darling! Only the cat.
(Fighty-bitey, ever-so-mighty)
Out in the moony dark.

Mother, Mother, what was that?
Hush, my darling! Only the cat.
(Prowly-yowly, sleepy-creepy,
Fighty-bitey, ever-so-mighty)
Out in the moony dark.

Mother, Mother, what was that?
Hush, my darling! Only the cat.
(Sneaky-peeky, cosy-dozy,
Prowly-yowly, sleepy-creepy,
Fighty-bitey, ever-so-mighty)
Out in the moony dark.

Mother, Mother, what was that?
Hush, my darling! Only the cat.
(Patchy-scratchy, furry-purry,
Sneaky-peeky, cosy-dozy,
Prowly-yowly, sleepy-creepy,
Fighty-bitey, ever-so-mighty)
Out in the moony dark.

Margaret Mahy

Old Jumpety-Bumpety-Hop-and-
Go-One
Was lying asleep on his side in the
sun.
This old kangaroo, he was whisking
the flies
(With his long glossy tail) from his
ears to his eyes.
Jumpety-Bumpety-Hop-and-Go-One
Was lying asleep on his side in the
sun,
Jumpety-Bumpety-Hop!

Anon

134

8th

Muhammad's Birthday

Far-flung families meet,
aunties, uncles and cousins
greet and kiss one another
on the cheek.

The table groans with bowls
of food, far more than I
can ever eat;
with jugs of lassi
and lemon sherbert,
to help wash down
the sticky sweets.

And there are many other treats.
New clothes to wear
for the musical procession
round the streets,
a walk that makes me feel
so glad
to celebrate the birthday
of Muhammad.

After our visit to the mosque,
fireworks light up the dusk
and we give thanks and pray
for a very special sort of day.
Then, tired but happy,
I climb into bed
with birthday memories singing
softly in my head.

Jim Hatfield

The Fly-Away Horse

Oh, a wonderful horse is the Fly-
　Away Horse –
Perhaps you have seen him
　before;
Perhaps, while you slept, his
　shadow has swept
Through the moonlight that floats
　on the floor.
For it's only at night, when the
　stars twinkle bright,
That the Fly-Away Horse, with a
　neigh
And a pull at his rein and a toss of
　his mane,
　　Is up on his heels and away!
　　　The Moon in the sky,
　　　As he gallopeth by,
　　Cries: "Oh! what a
　　　marvellous sight!"
　　　And the Stars in dismay
　　　Hide their faces away
　　In the lap of old
　　　Grandmother Night.

It is yonder out yonder, the Fly-
　Away Horse
Speedeth ever and ever away –
Over meadows and lanes, over
　mountains and plains,

Over streamlets that sing at their
　play;
And over the sea like a ghost
　sweepeth he,
While the ships they go sailing
　below,
And he speedeth so fast that the
　men at the mast
Adjudge him some portent of woe.
　"What ho, there!" they cry,
　　As he flourishes by
With a whisk of his beautiful tail;
　And the fish in the sea
　Are as scared as can be,
From the nautilus up to the whale!

And the Fly-Away Horse seeks
　those far-away lands
You little folk dream of at night –
Where candy-trees grow, and
　honey-brooks flow,
And corn-fields with popcorn are
　white;
And the beasts in the wood are
　ever so good
To children who visit them there –
What glory astride of a lion to
　ride,
Or to wrestle around with a bear!

The monkeys, they say:
"Come on, let us play,"
And they frisk in the coconut-trees:
While the parrots that cling
To the peanut-vines, sing
Or converse with comparative ease!

Off! Scamper to bed – you shall
ride him tonight!
For, as soon as you've fallen asleep,
With jubilant neigh he shall bear
you away
Over forest and hillside and deep!
But tell us, my dear, all you see and
you hear
In those beautiful lands over there,
Where the Fly-Away Horse wings
his far-away course
With the wee one consigned to his
care.
Then Grandma will cry
In amazement: "Oh, my!"
And she'll think it could never be so.
And only we two
Shall know it is true –
You and I, little precious! shall
know!

Eugene Field

10th

Overtaken by the Dark

Overtaken by the dark,
The shade beneath a tree
I make my inn;
And tonight my host
Shall be a flower.

Taira Tadanori
Translated by Geoffrey Bownas and
Anthony Thwaite

11th

Prayer

Please –
　　Help Mummy
　　　with her music
　　Uncle with his bus
　　Daddy with his writing
　　Grandma far away...
　　Help soldiers
　　　nurses
　　　puppies
　　all children as they play
　　　but most of all
　　　help Rovers
　　　to win
　　　on Saturday.

Peter Dixon

12th

Sunning

Old Dog lay in the summer sun
Much too lazy to rise and run.
He flapped an ear
At a buzzing fly;
He winked a half-opened
Sleepy eye;
He scratched himself
On an itching spot;
As he dozed on the porch
When the sun was hot.
He whimpered a bit
From force of habit,
While he lazily dreamed
Of chasing a rabbit.
But Old Dog happily lay in the sun,
Much too lazy to rise and run.

James S. Tippett

13th

The Wriggly Itches

I've got the wriggly itches,
I can't keep still to sleep,
The bed is full of popcorn,
There's toffee on the sheet.

    It's hot in here, far too hot
    And I'm in an awful sweat,
    The pillow's gone all lumpy
    And the sheet is sopping wet.

The duvet's flopped off to the floor
And rolled into a hump,
There's something buzzing in my
   ear,
And it's made an itchy lump.

    I keep on twisting over,
    My body wants to turn,
    There must be something
       inside me
    That thinks I am a worm.

I know I'll never get to sleep,
   It really is a pain.
What d'you mean, *It's morning* –
   Time to get up again?

Ivan Jones

14th

Late Night Caller

The tick of the clock,
the click of the lock,
a shoeless sock
on the stair,

the groan of the floor,
the squeak of a door,
the sigh of a drawer –
who's there?

A current of air,
a pencil of light –
"I'm back, son. All right?
Good night!"

Sue Cowling

15th

The Night Tree

When Elizabeth lies in her bed at
    night, she can gaze out into a tree.
And there are things in its leaves
    and branches that only she can
    see.
The tree stands in her window, like
    a picture in a frame.
But night after night as she looks
    at it, the picture is never the
    same.

On moonshiny nights Elizabeth
    sees a moonbird alight in her
    tree.
A preening, pearly-tailed moonbird
    from a faraway galaxy.
She can see its moon-blue plumage
    and the moonstones aglow on its
    wings.
She can hear the soft and silvery
    sound of the moonsong that it
    sings.

On windblown nights Elizabeth
    sees a galleon a-sail in her tree.
A swooping, storm-tossed galleon
    riding a white-crested sea.
She can see the sails flap and flurry
    and the brave flags flying on
    high.
She can hear the creak of the
    mighty masts and the wild wind's
    whooping cry.

On rainwashed nights Elizabeth
    sees a palace built high in her
    tree.
A glittering, glass and gilt palace
    with gates of chalcedony.
She can see the shimmer of
    chandeliers shining out from
    turrets and towers.
She can hear the music of fountain-
    splash gentle as summer showers.

On snow-silent nights Elizabeth
    sees a leopard prowling her tree.
A snow-white, silky-sleek leopard
    with paws padding stealthily.
She can see the snowflake markings
    that marble his glossy coat.
She can hear the deep, purring
    promises that rumble in his
    throat.

140

When Elizabeth wakes in the
morning, she gazes out
    into her tree.
And its friendly leaves and
    branches are all that she
    can see.
Elizabeth's tree is just a tree when
    she looks at it in the light.
But the wonders, the marvels, the
    mysteries she sees in her tree at
    night!

Carol Ann Martin

16th

Last Night I Dreamed
of Chickens

Last night I dreamed of chickens,
there were chickens everywhere,
they were standing on my stomach,
they were nesting in my hair,
they were pecking at my pillow,
they were hopping on my head,
they were ruffling up their feathers
as they raced about my bed.
They were on the chairs and tables,
they were on the chandeliers,
they were roosting in the corners,
they were clucking in my ears,
there were chickens, chickens,
  chickens
for as far as I could see...
when I woke today, I noticed
there were eggs on top of me.

Jack Prelutsky

17th

Painting the Moon

The moon's
A floating football
In the sky,
A yellow melon
Way up high,
A toffee round
And wrapped in gold,
An Olympic medal
Big and bold.
Reach up!
Grab hold!

Patricia Leighton

18th

Who Spoke?

Who spoke?
"Croak! Croak!
We spoke,
Frogs from the pond,
The still, cool pond,
That we've leaped beyond.

And now that the sun has set
And the sky's dark as jet
We are deep in grass made wet

By cool washes and sloshes of rain,
Rivers and slivers of rain,
Buckets of bountiful rain.

What bliss to be
So moist and so free.
We croak continually."

Olive Dove

Badger

Through the trees I saw a badger
In the evening, nearly dusk
All the midges dancing round me
Foxglove scent, and ferny musk.

Through the trees I saw a badger
In the twilight, stars just out
Bats like rags were drifting,
    swooping
Sheep on hillside, farmer's shout.

Through the trees I saw a badger
Through the air as grey as smoke
Light as dancers she came listening
Light as ghosts she sniffed the dark.

Through the trees I saw a badger
Barred head lifted, wary, keen,
Then she faded through the
    bracken
Like a whisper, like a dream.

Berlie Doherty

Catapillow

A catapillow
is a useful pet

To keep
upon your bed

Each night you simply
fluff him up

Then rest
your weary head.

Roger McGough

21st

Two Funny Men

I know a man
Who's upside down,
And when he goes to bed
His head's not on the pillow, No!
His *feet* are there instead.

I know a man
Who's back to front,
The strangest man *I've* seen.
He can't tell where he's going to
But he knows where he has been.

Spike Milligan

22nd

Before the Beginning

Sometimes in dreams I imagine
Alone and unafraid
I'm standing in the darkness
When the first bright stars were
    made.

When the sun sprang out of the
    blackness
And lit the world's first dawn
When torrents of rock rained
    upwards
And the mountains and seas were
    born.

And I'm there when the forests and
    meadows
Flowered for the very first time
When eyeless legless creatures
Oozed upwards out of the slime.

But when I awake and read the
    books
Though they tell me more and
    more
The one thing they never tell me
Is – what was there before...

Gareth Owen

24th

To Bed, to Bed

To bed, to bed,
Says Sleepyhead.
Tarry a while,
Says Slow.
Put on the pan,
Says Greedy Nan,
Let's sup before
We go.

Anon

23rd

H25

Hedgehogs hog the hedges
roadhogs hog the roads:
I'd like to build a motorway
for badgers, frogs and toads,
with halts for hungry hedgehogs
at an all-night service station;
four lanes wide and free from man
right across the nation.
Free from oil and petrol fumes,
and free from motor-cars
to see the busy hedgehogs trot
underneath the stars.

Adrian Henri

25th

Moony, Moony, Macaroony

Moony, moony,
Macaroony –
Pour the darkness,
Dunk it in!

Starry, starry,
Pickle-jarry –
Spear a little
Silverskin!

Sue Cowling

26th

Tell Me Why

There are so many different
   questions!
Do you know what I want to
   know?
Why does a cricket sing?
And where do the dodos go?

How big is a rattlesnake's rattle?
And what makes a grasshopper
   hop?
Do frogs leap-frog over each other?
The questions I ask never stop.

When a bat wants to see in the
   dark
does it carry a torch on its head?
Why do fireflies flicker at night
only after I've gone to bed?

Can a humming bird hum in tune?
Do flying fish fly in the sky?
When I close my eyes I fall fast
   asleep.
Won't somebody tell me...?

Cicely Herbert

27th

Night

Night crept like a smuggler
through town,
put the park
in his enormous sack,
swung his star-lined cape
over houses, church and beck,
then as people slept,
stole away
to his silvery dream-ship.

Joan Poulson

28th

What to Take to Bed in Summer

When I go to bed in Winter
I like to take a hotty.
But when I go in Summer
A hotty would be potty.
In Summer so much better
To take a cube of ice
And slide it round your mouth –
It's really twice as nice!

Ivan Jones

29th

The Squeak

I've got a teddy.
He cannot speak.
But in his tummy
he has a squeak.

He can't say, "No."
He can't say, "Yes."
But he always answers
when I press.

Have you heard
my teddy squeak?
Ready, teddy?
Steady...
EEEEEK!

Tony Mitton

JULY
30th & 31st

30th

In a Wonderland

A boat, beneath a sunny sky
Lingering onward dreamily
In an evening of July –

Children three that nestle near,
Eager eye and willing ear,
Pleased a simple tale to hear –

In a Wonderland they lie,
Dreaming as the days go by,
Dreaming as the summers die:

Ever drifting down the stream –
Lingering in the golden gleam –
Life, what is it but a dream?

Lewis Carroll

31st

Magic in the Moonlight

There's a magic in the moonlight,
I can feel it in the air;
There are glow-worms in the garden,
I can see them everywhere;
There's a shimmering reflection
On the surface of the pond;
There's a fairy by the fountain
With her tiny magic wand.

As I'm peeping through my curtains,
She is whispering my name;
She is calling me to join her
In a secret fairy game;
Now I'm floating through the window
And my body feels so light,
Soon we're dancing on a moonbeam
In the middle of the night.

And then she feeds me sweet fruits
That fairy people grow,
And whispering the secrets
That only fairies know,
At last she leads me by the hand,
And then to my delight,
She tucks me up in bed again
And kisses me goodnight.

Mike Jubb

AUGUST
1st – 31st

Tyger, tyger, burning bright
In the forests of the night...

I Met at Eve

I met at eve the Prince of Sleep,
His was a still and lovely face,
He wandered through a valley
 steep,
  Lovely in a lonely place.

His garb was grey of lavender,
About his brows a poppy-wreath
Burned like dim coals, and every-
 where
  The air was sweeter for his
   breath.

His twilight feet no sandals wore,
His eyes shone faint in their own
 flame,
Fair moths that gloomed his steps
 before
  Seemed letters of his lovely
   name.

His house is in the mountain ways,
A phantom house of misty walls,
Whose golden flocks at evening
 graze,
  And 'witch the moon with
   muffled calls.

Upwelling from his shadowy
 springs
Sweet waters shake a trembling
 sound,
There flit the hoot-owl's silent
 wings,
  There hath his web the silk-
   worm wound.

Dark in his pools clear visions lurk,
And rosy, as with morning buds,
Along his dales of broom and birk
  Dreams haunt his solitary
   woods.

I met at eve the Prince of Sleep,
His was a still and lovely face,
He wandered through a valley
 steep,
  Lovely in a lonely place.

Walter de la Mare

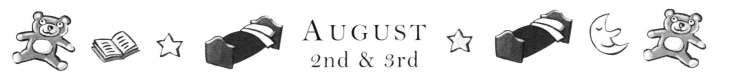
2nd

My Insect Dream

It must have been the lessons
Yesterday in school:
We did Music and Dancing
And they were pretty cool.
Then in the Science lesson,
"Insects" was the theme,
And they all got jumbled
In last night's dream...

First came a fly
With a violin,
Then a gnat
With a fancy hat
Joined in.
Beetles and mosquitoes
Whirled into the dance
And the fellows
Playing cellos –
Yes, I'm sure they were ants.
Next came a butterfly
And then a bee,
And last, with two extra legs,
Came me!

I checked my legs quickly
When I woke and – phew!
To my relief I'd still only got two.

Eric Finney

3rd

Good Night

The night is cold.
My bed is warm.
I hear outside
a sudden storm.

I hear the rain.
I feel the pillow.
I cuddle Teddy Tommy True
and Andy Armadillo.

I snuggle up against Bog Dog
and Ernest Bagwoof Bagwoof
  Brown
and drift away
to Sleepy Town,

I drift away to Sleepy Town,
I sleep away to Drifty Town,
To Drifty Town,
To Tifty Down,

I dreep away
to Tifty Town.

Fred Sedgwick

4th

On the Beach

Plastic windmills
  Whirling round;
Ghetto blasters'
Bellowing sound.
    Candy floss
All pink and sticky;
Trays with tea-cups
  (Very tricky)
Camera missing –
Under the heap...
    Uncle William
    Fast asleep.

John Coutts

5th

Only the Moon

When I was a child I thought
the new moon was a cradle
The full moon was granny's round
  face.

The new moon was a banana
The full moon was a big cake.

When I was a child
I never saw the moon
I only saw what I wanted to see.

And now I see the moon
It's the moon
Only the moon, and nothing but
  the moon.

Wong May
Translated by E.Thumboo

Granny and the Broomstick

Granny found the broom
When she was clearing out the
    shed.
"Just the job for sweeping up the
    garden!"
Granny said.

That night, as Granny lay in bed
With curlers in her hair,
She heard a crafty, creepy sound
Come swishing up the stairs.

The door swung wide, and some-
    thing tall
Came jumping in the room.
"Good gracious me!" cried Granny.
"It's a jumping, walking broom!"

When Granny touched the broom,
    they both
Went floating to the ceiling.
"It tickles!" chuckled Granny.
"What a most peculiar feeling!"

They flew out of the bedroom
With a roaring, soaring ZOOM!
"It's just as well you left that
    window open,"
Said the broom.

They flew as low as dustbin lids
And gave two cats a fright.
They flew as high as mountains
Up into the starry night.

"Fancy a trip to Timbuctoo?"
The broom asked. "Paris? Rome?"
"I'm feeling rather tired just now,"
    said Granny.
"Take me home."

The broom flew silently above
The dark and sleepy streets
And slipped the gently-snoring
    Granny
Back between her sheets.

When Granny woke next morning
And remembered all she'd seen,
She rubbed her eyes and said, "I've
    had
A funny sort of dream!

Imagine someone my age
On a broomstick – what a sight!"
But from then onwards, Granny
    dreamed
Of flying every night.

Andrew Matthews

7th

The Dream of a Girl Who Lived at Sevenoaks

Seven sweet singing birds up in a
tree;
Seven swift sailing-ships white
upon the sea;
Seven bright weathercocks shining
in the sun;
Seven slim racehorses ready for a
run;
Seven gold butterflies, flitting overhead;
Seven red roses blowing in a
garden bed;
Seven white lilies, with honey bees
inside them;

Seven round rainbows with clouds
to divide them;
Seven pretty little girls with sugar
on their lips;
Seven witty little boys, whom
everybody tips;
Seven nice fathers, to call little
maids "joys";
Seven nice mothers, to kiss the
little boys;
Seven nights running I dreamt it
all plain;
With bread and jam for supper I
could dream it all again!

William Brighty Rands

154

8th

Birthday Bike

For my birthday gift
I had a brand-new bike
With eighteen gears,
  Alloy wheels,
  Lights!

That night I should have slept
But found myself in Space.
I cycled past Mars
  To the stars,
  It was ace!

I didn't fall (not once)
Just kept on pedalling,
The spokes sparkling silver,
  The dark chain
  Humming.

I reached the Milky Way,
Whizzed up its spangled lanes,
Alone, but so happy!
  Then free-wheeled
  Down again.

Through my open window
I came riding in
Asleep, still in the saddle
  Just as dawn
  Was sliding in!

Ivan Jones

9th

from **In the Summer When I Go to Bed**

In the summer when I go to bed
The sun still streaming overhead
My bed becomes so small and hot
With sheets and pillow in a knot,
And then I lie and try to see
The things I'd really like to be.

I think I'd be a glossy cat
A little plump, but not too fat.
I'd never touch a bird or mouse
I'm much too busy round the
    house.

And then a fierce and hungry
    hound
The king of dogs for miles around;
I'd chase the postman just for fun
To see how quickly he could run.

Perhaps I'd be a crocodile
Within the marshes of the Nile
And paddle in the riverbed
With dripping mud-caps on my
    head.

Or maybe next a mountain goat
With shaggy whiskers at my
    throat,
Leaping streams and jumping rocks
In stripy pink and purple socks.

I'd like to be a tall giraffe
Making lots of people laugh,
I'd do a tap dance in the street
With little bells upon my feet.

But then before I really know
Just what I'd be or where I'd go
My bed becomes so wide and deep
And all my thoughts are fast
    asleep.

Thomas Hood

10th

Matthew, Mark, Luke and John

Matthew, Mark, Luke and John
Bless the bed that I lie on.
Four corners to my bed,
Four angels round my head,
  One to watch
  And one to pray
And two to keep me safe alway.

Anon

11th

Apple

Hi! I'm the apple round and red
that lives in the tree above your
  head.

It's my house, the leafy door
is open; branches make the floor.

Instead of clothes I wear the sun –
it's warm and silky on my skin.

My bath is cool rain from the sky,
the wind's the towel that rubs me
  dry;

through the night I sleep or wake
in the great blanket of the dark.

Shall I stay here? No, one day
you'll pick and eat me, so they say –

go ahead! Won't worry me –
my pips will grow another tree!

Lauris Edmond

12th

Krishna's Birthday

Krishna's Friends

As a boy, Lord Krishna
led His cow-herd friends
to the forest by the river
where all thought of toil ends.

Here we'll have our picnic,
where the sands are soft and clean
and the birds are chirping overhead
as sweetly as in a dream.

His friends, the little cow-herds,
ate in the open air,
near the lotus flowers,
with honey-bees humming there.

Later in the evening,
Krishna changed them like
    Himself –
Now they were clothed in yellow
    silk
and jewels of great wealth.

Every boy had four arms,
each wrist was braceleted
with shining golden bangles
and their heads were helmeted.

Their faces blue as rainclouds,
their smiles were filled with light
like the moon which shone above
    them
in the rosy skies of night.

Mal Lewis Jones

A Mime of Information

The mime is a story teller
whose tales are never heard
a funny man who can tell a joke
though he doesn't say a word.
He's an artist who needs no brush
to make pictures out of air
who, when he goes to bed at night,
climbs stairs that are not there!

Cicely Herbert

Tumbling

In jumping and tumbling
  We spend the whole day,
Till night by arriving
  Has finished our play.

What then? One and all,
  There's no more to be said,
As we tumbled all day,
  So we tumble to bed.

Anon

15th

Milk Boy

Each morning, before it was light,
The milk boy would wake
And walk out into the crisp dark.
The blue-grey van moved
Slowly, snail-slowly,
White pints stacked
Inside its shell.
The stars still out,
The clink and clank of glass.

And the day at last
breaking softly,
damp-nosed as a cow
breathing mist over a hedge.

And the milk boy
Hurrying in and out of the
    pathways,
leaving milk –
In and out like a sewing-machine,
Making little dab-stitches.

When he got to the bottom
Of the street
He'd look back at the doorsteps
And see the white thread
Of milk bottles
Glistening in the dawn.

Ivan Jones

16th

The Mouse in the Wainscot

Hush, Suzanne!
Don't lift your cup.
That breath you heard
Is a mouse getting up.

As the mist that steams
From your milk as you sup,
So soft is the sound
Of a mouse getting up.

There! did you hear
His feet pitter-patter,
Lighter than tipping
Of beads in a platter,

And then like a shower
On the window pane
The little feet scampering
Back again?

O falling of feather!
O drift of a leaf!
The mouse in the wainscot
Is dropping asleep.

Ian Serraillier

17th

Sleepy Sheep

I'm counting sheep
to go to sleep:
one, two, three.
The sheep are round my pillow.
They all belong to me.

I'm counting sheep
to go to sleep:
four, five, six.
They're dancing in the darkness
and playing funny tricks.

I'm counting sheep
to go to sleep:
seven, eight, nine.
And now I've started snoring,
so that's just fine.

Tony Mitton

18th

Blue Flashing Light

On the top of an ambulance
A blue flashing light
Travels like a shooting star
Fast through the night.

Here is an emergency,
Somewhere someone's ill,
The blue star is rushing
While the night stands still.

Celia Warren

19th

As the Old Russian Said

Sleep is a summer's
freedom

Slip into its hum
and haze

Drift away
like a bumblebee
nuzzling flowers

So many turns
of the path

So many miles
of blue...

Wander all night
for you will wake tireless

As the Old Russian said,

Go to sleep like a stone
Rise up like a loaf

Roger Garfitt

20th

The Weeper

All alone, alone I dwell,
Captive within my bony shell,
A hermit in a hermit's cell.

I have no feet, I cannot walk;
I have no tongue, I cannot talk;
But eyes I have, each on a stalk –

Their dazzling drops of sorrow fall
In glints of silver over all,
As, silken, beneath the moon, I
  crawl.

Across the grass at dawn you see,
Shimmering, my tearful tracery;
No other creature weeps like me!

Gina Wilson

21st

The Babes in the Wood

Listen, do you know,
How a long time ago,
  Two poor little children,
Whose names I don't know,
Were stolen away
On a fine summer's day,
  And left in a wood,
As I've heard people say.

Among the trees high,
Beneath the blue sky
  They plucked the bright flowers
And watched the birds fly;
Then on blackberries fed,
And strawberries red,
  And when they were weary,
"We'll go home," they said.

But they lost their way
At the end of the day;
  The moon gave no light
And the forest turned grey.
Then how they did weep
For someone to keep
  Them safe until morning,
While they lay down to sleep.

The birds overhead,
The robins so red
  Brought strawberry leaves
And over them spread.
They did what they could
To make a bed in the wood,
  And keep them from harm,
Those poor Babes in the Wood.

Traditional
Adapted by Mal Lewis Jones

164

22nd

The Tyger

Tyger! Tyger! burning bright
In the forests of the night,
What immortal hand or eye
Could frame thy fearful symmetry?

In what distant deeps or skies
Burnt the fire of thine eyes?
On what wings dare he aspire?
What the hand dare seize the fire?

And what shoulder, and what art,
Could twist the sinews of thy
    heart?
And when thy heart began to beat,
What dread hand? and what dread
    feet?

What the hammer? what the chain?
In what furnace was thy brain?
What the anvil? what dread grasp
Dare its deadly terrors clasp?

When the stars threw down their
    spears,
And water'd heaven with their
    tears,
Did he smile his work to see?
Did he who made the Lamb make
    thee?

Tyger! Tyger! burning bright
In the forests of the night,
What immortal hand or eye,
Dare frame thy fearful symmetry?

William Blake

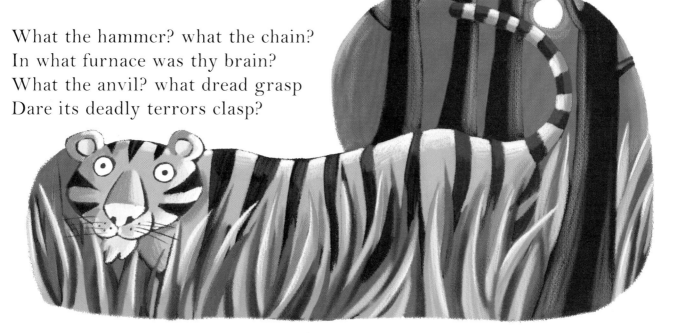

23rd

Bat Chant

I'm a bat
furry bat
and I'm happy as Larry in the dark
'Cos I got radar, I don't need
    eyesight
I dip and I loop
In the dovegray twilight
I zip and I swoop
in the navyblue midnight
but I'm over the moon when it's
    black as pitch.
Come the dawn I'll be gone
but at sunset I start to twitch
when my folded up wings begin to
    itch
for the dark,
pitch dark.
No I'm not a
spooky moth, no I'm not a
sort of
night bird not a flying mouse
though I fly and I squeak in my
    hollowtree house
I'm a bat
fancy that,
highnoon
I hang upside down like a sunny
    day umbrella
waiting for dark

wait till night is as
dark as the big black cloak of
    Dracula
I'm a bat
I'm unique
from my highpitch unaided hearing
and my supersonic squeak
I'm a bat
and I'm happy as Larry in the dark.

Liz Lochhead

24th

25th

A Spell for Sleeping

slumbering lullaby butterfly dream
silvery summery watery day
magical musical kingfisher stream
whispering secrets and flying away

Sleep tight my darling
Dream of happy things
No harm can come to you
Let your dreams have wings

Mike Jubb

In the bath

In the bath
   you can swim,
      you can swim,
         you can swim, swim, swim!

You can swim a wide river,
you can swim across a lake.
You can swim in the ocean,
like a haddock or a hake.
You can swim to an island,
or swim the stormy seas.
In the bath you can swim
just any time you please.

In the bath
   you can swim,
      you can swim,
         you can swim, swim, swim!

Wes Magee

26th

Sea Bed

My blue curtains
make it seem to me
that my new bedroom
is under the sea.

Far above the ceiling,
way up there,
I can imagine
boats, birds, air.

But down in my sea bed
I dream and read,
surrounded by fish
and rocks and weed.

Tony Mitton

27th

It Gets Dark

The crescent moon
is a slick snake
which has come too soon.
The sunset is fading
like my flowery sundress.
It is not dark yet.

Now a very old blanket
with starry holes in it
is covering the sky.
The sun on the other side
is begging to get through.

The trees are lurking.
It gets dark.

Laura Ranger (8)

28th

The Friday Night Smell

I love the
friday night
smell of
mammie baking
bread – creeping
up to me in
bed, and tho
zzz I'll fall
asleep, before I
even get a
bite – when
morning comes,
you can bet
I'll meet a
kitchen table
laden with
bread, still
warm and fresh
salt bread
sweet bread
crisp and brown
& best of all
coconut buns
THAT's why
I love the
friday night
smell of mammie
baking bread
putting me to

sleep, dreaming
of jumping from
the highest branch
of the jamoon tree
into the red water
creek
beating carlton
run & catching
the biggest fish
in the world
plus, getting
the answers right
to every single
sum
that every day
in my dream
begins and ends
with the friday
night smell of
mammie baking
bread, and
coconut buns
of course.

Marc Matthews

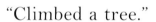
29th

This and That

Two cats together
In bee-heavy weather
After the August day
In smug contentment lay
By the garden shed
In the flower bed
Yawning out the hours
In the shade of the flowers
And passed the time away,
Between stretching and washing
    and sleeping,
Talking over the day.

"Climbed a tree."
"Aaaah."
"Terrorized sparrows."
"Mmmmh."
"Was chased."
"Aaaah."
"Fawned somewhat!"
"Mmmmh."
"Washed, this and that,"
Said the first cat.

And they passed the time away
Between stretching and washing
    and sleeping
Talking over the day.

"Gazed out of parlour window."
"Aaaah."
"Pursued blue bottles."
"Mmmmh."
"Clawed curtains."
"Aaaah."
"Was cuffed."
"Mmmmh."
"Washed, this and that,"
Said the other cat.

And they passed the time away
Between stretching and washing
  and sleeping
Talking over the day.

"Scratched to be let in."
"Aaaah."
"Patrolled the house."
"Mmmmh."
"Scratched to go out."
"Aaaah."
"Was booted."
"Mmmmh."
"Washed, this and that,"
Said the first cat.

And they passed the time away
Between stretching and washing
  and sleeping
Talking over the day.

"Lapped cream elegantly."
"Aaaah."
"Disdained dinner."
"Mmmmh."
"Borrowed a little salmon."
"Aaaah."
"Was tormented."
"Mmmmh."
"Washed, this and that,"
Said the other cat.

And they passed the time away
Between stretching and washing
  and sleeping
Talking over the day.

Gareth Owen

30th

Holiday Dreams

Dream of an ice-cream
Tall as a mountain
Shot through with strawberries
And chocolate chips

Dream of a pool
With a lemonade fountain
Soda pop whirlpool
And cool Pepsi dips

Dream of a beach
With sand-golden honey
Lollipop sunshades
And liquorice caves

Dream you will be there
Tomorrow, by sunset,
Paddling your toes
In champagne waves.

Patricia Leighton

31st

O Moon!

O Moon! when I look on your
beautiful face
Careering along through the
darkness of space,
The thought has frequently come
to my mind,
If I'll ever gaze on your lovely
behind.

Anon

SEPTEMBER
1st – 30th

The Sleep-Stealer wears dancing shoes,
   He slips through cracks and chimney-flues...

1st

Song of the Big Toe

Heigh ho,
Big toe,
To and fro,
Nice and slow.

Pick me up,
Swing me high,
Big toe
Won't cry.

Into bed,
In we go,
Bye, bye,
Big toe.

Wendy Cope

2nd

The Farmer's Shadow

Soft is the farmer's shadow
Upon the golden corn,
As we set off a-harvesting
In the early morn.

Swift is the farmer's shadow
When work is to be done,
The straw we bundle into sheaves
In the midday sun.
Long is the farmer's shadow
As we all make our way
Along the path that takes us home
At the end of day.

Colin West

3rd

"It's Time For Bed, You Know"

When I'm desperate to find the
    answer
To something I do not know
Mum says, "Ask your father."
He says, "It's time for bed, you
    know."

"Why does the world spin so
    slow?"
"It's time for bed, you know."

"Why don't fireflies always glow?"
"It's time for bed, you know."

"Why don't owls or pigeons crow?"
"It's time for bed, you know."

I went to a library,
Picked a book called *Learn and
    Grow*
Just when I chose to open it
Dad winked, "It's time for bed, you
    know."

There must be a better ploy
For staying up late to see
The movies I'm not supposed to
    watch
On video and TV...

Brian Patten

The Sleep-Stealer

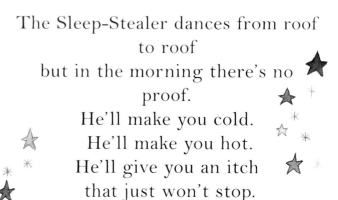

The Sleep-Stealer wears dancing
shoes.
He slips through cracks and
chimney-flues,
and he won't steal your money
or peep under your sheet.
He doesn't hurt anyone,
but he does steal sleep.

The Sleep-Stealer's shuffle is light
but sure.
He'll tickle the window and rattle
the door,
and just when your eyes
fill with flickers of sleep,
he'll set off a car-alarm
out in the street.

The Sleep-Stealer's got a bag full
of worries.
He scatters them down, then off he
hurries.
They slip through your mind
like bits of confetti
and make you remember
what you were forgetting.

The Sleep-Stealer dances from roof
to roof
but in the morning there's no
proof.
He'll make you cold.
He'll make you hot.
He'll give you an itch
that just won't stop.

But the Sleep-Stealer's really
easy to beat.
There's no need for daft things like
counting sheep.
Just close your eyes,
snuggle your feet,
think of your dreams,
and breathe deep...

Close your eyes,
snuggle your feet,
think of your dreams,
and breathe deep...

Close your eyes,
snuggle your feet,
think of your dreams,
and sleep.

Sean Taylor

5th

Fairies

There are fairies at the bottom of
  our garden!
  It's not so very, very far away;
You pass the gardener's shed and
  you just keep straight ahead –
  I do so hope they've really come to
    stay.
There's a little wood, with moss in
  it and beetles,
  And a little stream that quietly
    runs through;
You wouldn't think they'd dare to
  come merry-making there –
    Well, they do.

There are fairies at the bottom of
  our garden!
  They often have a dance on
    summer nights;
The butterflies and bees make a
  lovely little breeze,
  And the rabbits stand about and
    hold the lights.
Did you know that they could sit
  upon the moonbeams

And pick a little star to make a
  fan,
And dance away up there in the
  middle of the air?
    Well, they can.

There are fairies at the bottom of
  our garden!
  You cannot think how beautiful
    they are;
They all stand up and sing when
  the Fairy Queen and King
  Come gently floating down upon
    their car.
The King is very proud and *very*
  handsome;
  The Queen – now can you guess
    who that could be
(She's a little girl all day, but at
  night she steals away)?
    Well – it's me!

Rose Fyleman

177

6th

The Sleep Train

The Sleep Train is coming,
　bringing the night.
The stars are out, tuck in tight.

It hoots like an owl and it's painted
　night-black
and it's rushing here with a
　clickety-clack,
　　clickety-clack,

bringing bedtime stories and bed-
　time rhymes,
so that you're ready for tomorrow's
　playtimes.

Now it's time to get on, time to get
　on,
time you were gone,
　time you were gone.

Fall fast asleep, fall fast asleep
and don't peep, don't peep,
　don't peep.

Tim Pointon

7th

Good Night

A fair little girl sat under a tree,
Sewing as long as her eyes could
　see;
Then smoothed her work, and
　folded it right,
And said, "Dear work! Good Night!
　Good Night!"

Such a number of rooks came over
　her head,
Crying "Caw! Caw!" on their way to
　bed;
She said, as she watched their
　curious flight,
"Little black things, Good Night!
　Good Night!"

Richard Monckton Milnes

8th

I Will Not Fall Asleep

Last night as I lay in my bed
A warm and cosy heap
I made myself a promise
That I would not fall asleep.

Yes I made myself a promise
That I truly meant to keep
That no matter what might happen
I would not fall asleep.

I'd count the hours on the clock
I'd listen to the cars
I'd do long divisions in my head
And add up all the stars.

I'd tell my eyelids not to droop
And speak sharply to my eyes
And prop them open with my
    thumbs
Till the sun began to rise.

And what would they say at school,
    I thought
When I told them during break
That while they all were sleeping
I lay wide awake.

I'd tell them all, "It's easy,
All you do is keep

Both your eyes stuck open wide
And you'll never fall asleep."

"No you'll never fall asleep," I'd say,
"Your eyes will never droop
If you keep on saying to yourself
I will not fall asloop."

"Yes never ever sloop a fall
Always wape akeep
If you keep on zaying to youzself
I will
not
fall a
ah
ah
ah
z z z z z z z z z z z z z z
zzzzzzzzzzzzzzzzzzzzzzzzzzzz
zzzzzzzzzzzzz"

Gareth Owen

179

9th

A Path to the Moon

From my front door there's a path
   to the moon
that nobody seems to see
tho it's marked with stones &
   grass and trees
there's nobody sees it but me.

You walk straight ahead for ten
   trees or so
turn left at the robin's song
follow the sound of the west wind
   down
past where the deer drink from the
   pond.

You take a right turn as the river
   bends
then where the clouds touch the
   earth
close your left eye & count up to
   ten
while twirling for all that you're
   worth.

And if you keep walking right
   straight ahead
clambering over the clouds
saying your mother's & father's
   names
over & over out loud

you'll come to the place where
   moonlight's born
the place where the moonbeams
   hide
and visit all of the crater sites
on the dark moon's secret side.

From my front door there's a path
   to the moon
that nobody seems to see
tho it's marked with stones & grass
   & trees
no one sees it but you & me.

b.p. Nichol

SEPTEMBER
10th & 11th

Our New Arrivals

Snoozing, snuffling, twitching,
   dreaming,
Our five black puppies
Sleep.

Yawning, stretching, grunting,
   rolling,
Our five black puppies
Wake.

Jumping, squealing, running,
   gumming,
Our five black puppies
Play.

Sniffing, sucking, lapping, spilling,
Our five black puppies
Eat.

Snoozing, snuffling, twitching,
   dreaming,
Our five black puppies
Sleep.

Oliver Hilton-Johnson (9)

Night Bird

At night,
I fly upstairs, I don't walk.
Why?
Because I'm a bird.
No you're not.
Can't you see my wings,
Folded neatly behind me?
I don't need them just now.
So, what do you find
When you reach your bed?
A nest of twigs and moss and straw
And, in the centre, a soft hollow
   made of down.
And when the wind blows through
   my room,
I rock in my safe downy hollow,
And gaze at the moon.

Jenny Nimmo

12th

Hushabye Lullaby

Listen. Hush.
Don't be hasty.
Something's eating
Something tasty.

In the cupboard
As lights go off
Can't you hear
Moths chomping cloth?

Listen. Hush.
Other sounds
Are moonlight falling
On the ground,

And shadows bumping
Into trees,
And the snoring,
Dreaming bees.

Listen. Hush.
Isn't that
The soft pad
Of the cat?

There are sounds
I am not sure
I have ever
Heard before.

I try so hard
To hear all things
Behind the silence
That sleep brings.

Brian Patten

13th

from **I Wish I Were...**

Just as it gets dark in the evening
    and my mother sends me to bed,
I can see through the open window
    the watchman walking up and
        down.
The lane is dark and lonely, and the
    street-lamp stands
Like a giant with one red eye in its
    head.
The watchman swings his lantern
    and walks with his
        shadow at his side, and never
        once goes to bed in his life.
I wish I were a watchman walking
    the streets all night, chasing the
        shadows with my lantern.

Rabindranath Tagore

14th

Thank-You Letter

Dear Sun,
Just a line to say:
Thanks for this
And every day.
Your dawns and sunsets
Are just great –
Bang on time,
Never late.
On dismal days,
As grey as slate,
Behind a cloud
You calmly wait,
Till out you sail
With cheerful grace
To put a smile
On the world's face.
Thanks for those
Blazing days on beaches,
For ripening apples,
Pears and peaches;
For sharing out
Your noble glow;
For sunsets – the
Loveliest things I know.
Please carry on:
We know your worth.

Love from
    A Friend on Planet Earth.

Eric Finney

15th

As to the Restless Brook

Do you suppose the babbling brook
    Would stop and rest its head
If someone got a scoop and took
    The pebbles from its bed?

John Kendrick Bangs

16th

The Babysitter

When Mum and Dad go out
and it's time for bed,
the babysitter looks after us
instead.

So when we hear them go,
as they shut the gate,
we sneak downstairs and ask,
"Can we stay up late?"

Tony Mitton

17th

Where Are You Going, Jenny?

Where are you going, Jenny,
Dressed in green?

I'm going to the palace
To dine with the Queen.

Where are you going, Jenny,
Dressed in red?

I'm going for a ride
On Santa's sled.

Where are you going, Jenny,
Dressed in blue?

I'm going to have tea
With a kangaroo.

Where are you going, Jenny,
Dressed in white?

I'm going for a sail
On the ship of the night.

John Foster

Bedmobile

I hear my grandad on the stair
He's counting, One Two Three
Bringing a rosy apple plucked
From my special climbing tree.
He brings the garden in with him
The flowers and the air
And there are twigs and petals
Tangled in his hair.
And as I eat my apple
He sits down next to me
Turning an imaginary wheel.
"Where to today?" says he.
And we drive our deluxe Bedmobile
To school along the heath
With the apple dribbling sweetness
Clenched between my teeth.

Gareth Owen

18th

Dream Catcher

Over my bed is a delicate net
woven of silky silver thread.
Its tiny glass beads
bright raindrops are
and the gem in its centre
glows like a star.

A magical spider's web,
it is there
to trap evil dreams
and keep me from care.
But the good dreams
it sprinkles down on my head
so I dream in peace
in my soft, warm bed.

Patricia Leighton

20th

Badgers

Badgers come creeping from dark
   under ground,
Badgers scratch hard with a bristly
   sound,
Badgers go nosing around.

Badgers have whiskers and black
   and white faces,
Badger cubs scramble and scrap
   and run races,
Badgers like overgrown places.

Badgers don't jump when a vixen
   screams,
Badgers drink quietly from moonshiny streams,
Badgers dig holes in our dreams.

Badgers are working while you and
   I sleep,
Pushing their tunnels down
   twisting and steep,
Badgers have secrets to keep.

Richard Edwards

21st

Granny Granny Please Comb My Hair

Granny Granny
please comb my hair
you always take your time
you always take such care

You put me to sit on a cushion
between your knees
you rub a little coconut oil
parting gentle as a breeze

Mummy Mummy
she's always in a hurry-hurry rush
she pulls my hair
sometimes she tugs

But Granny
you have all the time in the world
and when you're finished
you always turn my head and say
"Now who's a nice girl."

Grace Nichols

186

23rd

Sun Dog, Star Bird, Moon Cat

A sun dog
runs down Beacon Hill
as the planets
tint the twilight.

A star bird
perches in a tree
as the moon cat
paws the skylight.

John Rice

22nd

Power Cut

The computer's not working,
The TV screen's blank;
The Teletext's vanished –
We've a POWER CUT to thank!

Can't video programmes
To watch later on;
The CD stopped playing
Halfway through a song;
The heating's not heating;
The cooker can't cook;
So I'm off to bed early
With a poetry book –

And a torch!

Trevor Harvey

24th

Moving

The van has gone.
The notice saying SOLD
Is taken down.
The family, weary, strained,
Begins to settle,
Uncomfortable, in the house
Not yet their home.
Tear-stained and lonely
The youngest boy escapes
Into the garden,
Presses his back for comfort
Against the plum tree's
Blackly knobbled bark.

A splutter of dry leaves.
A shiver through the long grass,
And then the hedgehog comes.
Scuttering, uncertain,
Pushing through the daisies
A mere heart's beat away.
It stops, nose twitching,
Scents the evening air –
And rests a moment,
Still, and unafraid.

The boy watches,
Smiles, and feels his pain
Retreat. "All right,"
He thinks. "This place will be
All right. Perhaps...
I'll LIKE it here."

Jennifer Curry

25th

Questions Before Going to Sleep

Tell me...
Is it easy to make thunder?
And when will the birds' nests be
    ripe?
How does the wind whistle his
    song?
And where does the raven sleep at
    night?
And above all, that rain I'm seeing,
Up in Heaven, are they weeing?

Frantisek Halas
Translated by Vera Fusek Peters and
Andrew Fusek Peters

26th

Sea Fever

I must go down to the seas again,
   to the lonely sea and the sky,
And all I ask is a tall ship and a
   star to steer her by,
And the wheel's kick and the
   wind's song and the white sail's
   shaking,
And a grey mist on the sea's face
   and a grey dawn breaking.

I must go down to the seas again,
   for the call of the running tide
Is a wild call and a clear call that
   may not be denied;
And all I ask is a windy day with
   the white clouds flying,
And the flung spray and the blown
   spume, and the sea-gulls crying.

I must go down to the seas again,
   to the vagrant gypsy life,
To the gull's way and the whale's
   way where the wind's like a
   whetted knife;
And all I ask is a merry yarn from
   a laughing fellow-rover,
And quiet sleep and a sweet dream
   when the long trick's over.

John Masefield

27th

Holy Day

The candle light is glowing
The children, fast asleep
Sound of voices humming
   Resonant and deep.

Yom Kippur, the Holiest Sabbath
   Celebrates the past
No food to be consumed
From sunset, we must fast.

So much to be remembered
A bond to bind us tight
   Safe, within the family
   God is strong tonight.

Sally Flood

28th

Kit's Cradle

They've taken the cosy bed away
That I made myself with the
    Shetland shawl,
And set me a hamper of scratchy
    hay,
By that great black stove in the
    entrance hall.

I won't sleep there; I'm resolved on
    that!
They may think I will, but they
    little know
There's a soft persistence about a
    cat
That even a little kitten can show.

I wish I knew what to do but pout,
And spit at the dogs and refuse my
    tea;
My fur's feeling rough, and I
    rather doubt
Whether stolen sausage agrees
    with me.

On the drawing-room soft they've
    closed the door,
They've turned me out of the easy-
    chairs;
I wonder it never struck me before
That they make their beds for
    themselves upstairs.

I've found a crib where they won't
    find me,
Though they're crying "Kitty!" all
    over the house.
Hunt for the Slipper! and riddle-
    my-ree!
A cat can keep as still as a mouse.

It's rather unwise perhaps to purr,
But they'll never think of the
    wardrobe-shelves.
I'm happy in every hair of my fur;
They may keep the hamper and hay
    themselves.

Juliana Horatia Ewing

29th

Nightlight

The toys on my bed like the light
    left on.
Ronnie the panda hates the dark.
Nibbles the velvet dog might bark
at the shadow hanging behind the
    door
which *I* know is only my dressing
    gown.
Carmelino, my patchwork clown
would think: now where's the day-
    light gone?

So the light shines out and I look
    at the things
that I've put near the lamp that's
    next to my bed.
There's an Action Man who's lost
    his head
and a couple of pieces of jigsaw sky,
a conker, some stamps, a rubber, a
    pen
and some wrinkled leaves that I
    found in my den
and a plastic eagle with wide,
    brown wings.

I'm not scared of the dark at all,
but Ronnie hates it, and Nibbles
    too
and Carmelino wouldn't sleep.
He'd flop down on to the pillow
    and weep
so I keep the lamp by my bed
    turned on
till morning comes and the night
    has gone
and the sun draws a line of gold on
    my wall.

Adèle Geras

30th

Greedy Green River

Now greedy green river has
    swallowed the sun,
Timid as twilight, the night
    creatures come.

Splodgy scuttlers, reeking of slime,
Darters, and burrowers with
    luminous eyes,
Scurrying twitterers, swoopers
    from trees,
With tails that tickle, or scales that
    gleam,
Or bristles that rustle like wind in
    dry leaves,

Timid as twilight, the night
    creatures come,
Now greedy green river has
    swallowed the sun.

Under the scum on duckweedy
    ponds
Frogspawn is foaming, tadpoles
    grow strong.
Toads creep stealthily out of the
    mud,
Crawl and wobble, and gobble the
    grubs.
Twigs flutter with moths. Bark
    oozes with slugs.

Timid as twilight, the night
    creatures come,
Now greedy green river has
    swallowed the sun.

Slow-worm wriggles his old bronze
    skin.
Water-rat plops like a furry fish,
Swimming and nosing his way
    through the reeds.
Hedgehog sniffs ditches itchy with
    fleas,
Then curls in a wasp-nest, and falls
    asleep.

Timid as twilight, the night
    creatures come,
Now greedy green river has
    swallowed the sun.

Leo Aylen

OCTOBER
1st – 31st

Tell me another story, Dad, tell me another tale.
Anything will do, Dad – dragon,
mermaid, whale...

 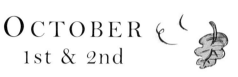 
1st

2nd

The Whale's Hymn

In an ocean before cold dawn broke
Covered by an overcoat
I lay awake in a boat
And heard a whale.

Hearing a song so solemn and so
    calm
It seemed absurd to feel alarm –
But I had a notion it sang
God's favourite hymn,

And spoke direct to Him.

Brian Patten

Bedtime Story

Tell me another story, Dad,
tell me another tale.
Anything will do, Dad –
dragon, mermaid, whale.

How the leopard
got its spots,
I really do like that one lots.

And how the elephant became,
I'd love to hear that one again.

Tell me how the stars
were made to shine
and why the sea is full of brine.

Tell me one of yours, Dad
and I'll tell you one of mine.

It is time to go to sleep,
my love.
I have told you four already.

Ah, but they were all for me, Dad.
Now could you tell one more
for Teddy?

Jim Hatfield

3rd

Dream Horses

I am the Dream Horse, black as
    night,
Climb in my saddle and hold on
    tight.
Ride with me now to the dark
    valley deep
That lies at the heart of the
    Mountains of Sleep.

I am the Dream Horse, fiery-red,
Showering sparks as I shake my
    head,
Taking you down through the
    stone caverns cold
Where dragons are sleeping in
    nests made of gold.

I am the Dream Horse, white as
    milk,
With jewels for eyes and a mane
    like silk.
I'll carry you safe to the end of the
    night,
Till you wake in your bed at the
    dawn's first light.

Andrew Matthews

4th

Garden Zoo

In my dream I had a garden zoo
with lions, tigers and a pink
    cockatoo.
Zebras and elephants were roaming
    there
while chimpanzees swung through
    the air.
Dolphins and seals swam to and
    from
the banks of the pond (turned
    aquarium).
An alligator, giraffe and a kangaroo
were there as guests in the garden
    too.
Now and then, the most colourful
    plants,
tempted a doctor bird to dance.
Then I fed the animals green
    calliloo,
yes they loved to eat green calliloo
and wash it down with red bean
    stew.
In my dream I had a garden zoo
will I dream of it tomorrow too... ?

Pauline Stewart

5th

The Song of Wandering Aengus

I went out to the hazel wood,
Because a fire was in my head,
And cut and peeled a hazel wand,
And hooked a berry to a thread,
And when white moths were on the
    wing,
And moth-like stars were flickering
    out,
I dropped the berry in a stream
And caught a little silver trout.

When I had laid it on the floor
I went to blow the fire a-flame,
But something rustled on the floor,
And someone called me by my
    name:
It had become a glimmering girl
With apple blossoms in her hair
Who called me by my name and
    ran
And faded through the brightening
    air.

Though I am old with wandering
Through hollow lands and hilly
    lands,
I will find out where she has gone,
And kiss her lips and take her
    hands;
And walk among long dappled
    grass,
And pluck till time and times are
    done,
The silver apples of the moon,
The golden apples of the sun.

William Butler Yeats

6th

Littlemouse

Light of day going,
Harvest moon glowing,
People beginning to snore,
Tawny owl calling,
Dead of night falling,
Littlemouse opening her door.

Scrabbling and tripping,
Sliding and slipping,
Over the ruts of the plough,
Under the field gate,
Mustn't arrive late,
Littlemouse hurrying now.

Into a clearing,
All the birds cheering,
Woodpecker blowing a horn,
Nightingale fluting,
Blackbird toot-tooting,
Littlemouse dancing till dawn.

7th

Night-lights

Three is no need to light a
        night-light
On a light night like tonight;
For a night-light's light's a
        slight light
When the moonlight's white
        and bright.

Anon

Soon comes the morning,
No time for yawning,
Home again Littlemouse creeps,
Over the furrow,
Back to her burrow,
Into bed. Littlemouse sleeps.

Richard Edwards

8th

Mr Fox O!

A fox jumped up one winter's
   night,
And begged the moon to give him
   light,
For he'd many miles to trot that
   night
Before he reached his den O!
   Den O! Den O!
For he'd many miles to trot that
   night
Before he reached his den O!

The first place he came to was a
   farmer's yard,
Where the ducks and the geese
   declared it hard
That their nerves should be shaken
   and their rest so marred
By a visit from Mr Fox O!
   Fox O! Fox O!
That their nerves should be shaken
   and their rest so marred
By a visit from Mr Fox O!

He took the grey goose by the
   neck,
And swung him right across his
   back;
The grey goose cried out, Quack,
   quack, quack,
With his legs hanging dangling
   down O!
   Down O! Down O!
The grey goose cried out, Quack,
   quack, quack,
With his legs hanging dangling
   down O!

Old Mother Slipper Slopper
   jumped out of bed,
And out of the window she popped
   her head:
Oh! John, John, John, the grey
   goose is gone,
And the fox is off to his den O!
   Den O! Den O!
Oh! John, John, John, the grey
   goose is gone,
And the fox is off to his den O!

The fox went back to his hungry
　　den,
And his dear little foxes, eight,
　　nine, ten;
Said they, Good daddy, you must go
　　there again,
If you bring such good cheer from
　　the farm O!
　　　Farm O! Farm O!
Said they, Good daddy, you must go
　　there again,
If you bring such good cheer from
　　the farm O!

The fox and his wife, without any
　　strife,
Said they never ate a better goose
　　in all their life:
They did very well without fork or
　　knife,
And the little ones picked the
　　bones O!
　　　Bones O! Bones O!
They did very well without fork or
　　knife,
And the little ones picked the
　　bones O!

Anon

9th

You Don't Frighten Me!

When I get frightened:

I stack,
I pack,
I pile,
I file
all my teddies around my bed.
And like soldiers at attention
they offer me a wall of protection.

Then I skip into my bed,
squeeze deep down into my duvet
and whisper,
"Come on Darkness,
you big, black, bullying,
bubble of trouble.
I'm ready with my teddies
and you don't frighten me!"

Ian Souter

10th

Five Eyes

In Hans' old mill his three black
   cats
Watch his bins for the thieving
   rats.
Whisker and claw, they crouch in
   the night,
Their five eyes smouldering green
   and bright:
Squeaks from the flour sacks,
   squeaks from where
The cold wind stirs on the empty
   stair,
Squeaking and scampering, every-
   where.
Then down they pounce, now in,
   now out,
At whisking tail, and sniffing
   snout;
While lean old Hans he snores
   away
Till peep of light at break of day;
Then up he climbs to his creaking
   mill,
Out come his cats all grey with
   meal –
Jekkel, and Jessup, and one-eyed
   Jill.

Walter de la Mare

11th

Night Ride

When I can't sleep
I shut my door
And sit on the rug
On my bedroom floor.

I open the window.
I close my eyes
And say magic words
Till my carpet flies:

Zooming over gardens,
Chasing after bats,
Hooting like an owl
And frightening the cats.

Then when I feel sleepy
And dreams are in my head,
I fly back through my window
And snuggle down in bed.

Celia Warren

12th

Ned

It's a singular thing that Ned
Can't be got out of bed.
    When the sun comes round
    He is sleeping sound
With the blankets over his head.
    They tell him to shunt,
    And he gives a grunt,
And burrows a little deeper –
    He's a trial to them
    At eight a.m.,
When Ned is a non-stop sleeper.

Oh, the snuggly bits
    Where the pillow fits
    Into his cheek and neck!
    Oh, the beautiful heat
    Stored under the sheet
Which the breakfast-bell will wreck!
Oo, the snoozly-oozly feel
He feels from head to heel,
    When to get out of bed
    Is worse to Ned
Than missing his morning meal!

But
It's a singular thing that Ned,
    After the sun is dead
    And the moon's come round,
    Is not to be found,
    And can't be got into bed!

Eleanor Farjeon

13th

The Man in the Moon

    The Man in the Moon
    Came down too soon
And asked the way to Norwich
    He went to the South
    And burned his mouth
By eating cold pease-porridge.

Anon

14th

Heaven

Your hair is golden on the pillow
And peace is in your lovely face.
Outside the starry night is shining,
The yellow moon is bright with
   grace.
All the world is spinning gently,
Heaven is here and everywhere.
As I kiss you softly, softly,
I pray you sleep without a care.

Ivan Jones

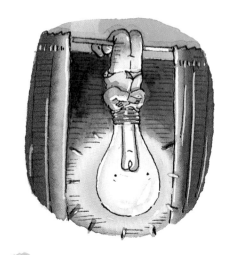

15th

Pearl

Pearl, Jemima
Alfreton-Hughes
Turned into a lightbulb
And blew her fuse
Out in the town
They noticed her plight
By the switch on her back
And her head burning bright
When she fell asleep
This light-hearted girl
Hung upside down
Like a fifty watt Pearl
"Please," begged Pearl
With a nervous cough,
*"Whatever you do
Don't switch me off."*

Gareth Owen

16th

Up the Stairs to Bedfordshire

Up the stairs to Bedfordshire.
That's what Daddy said.

Up the stairs to Sleepfordshire
to rest your little head.

Up the stairs to Dreamfordshire
and don't forget your Ted.

Up the stairs to Bedfordshire,
yes, up the stairs to bed.

Tony Mitton

17th

The Moon

The moon has a face like the clock
in the hall;
She shines on thieves on the garden
wall,
On streets and fields and harbour
quays,
And birdies asleep in the forks of
the trees.

The squalling cat and the
squeaking mouse,
The howling dog by the door of
the house,
The bat that lies in bed at noon,
All love to be out by the light of
the moon.

But all of the things that belong to
the day
Cuddle to sleep to be out of her
way;
And flowers and children close
their eyes
Till up in the morning the sun
shall rise.

Robert Louis Stevenson

18th

from The Bed Book

O who cares much
If a Bed's big or small
Or lumpy and bumpy –
Who cares at all

As long as its springs
Are bouncy and new.
From a Bounceable Bed
You bounce into the blue

Over the hollyhocks
(Toodle-oo!)
Over the owls'
To-whit-to-whoo,

Over the moon
To Timbuktoo
With springier springs
Than a kangaroo.

You can see if the Big Dipper's
Full of stew,
And you may want to stay
Up a week or two.

Sylvia Plath

19th

Here You Lie

Here you lie
    warm in bed,
feather pillow
    for your head.

In the dark
    town fox prowls,
brown owl swoops,
    guard dog growls.

In the dark
    cold winds blow,
tom cat creeps,
    white stars glow.

Here you lie
    warm in bed,
feather pillow
    for your head.

Wes Magee

20th

Autumn Leaves

Red leaves
gold leaves
get as loose
as my front teeth
then they fall out.

In Granny's garden
the tall oak tree
is as old as my mother.
It makes a red leaf carpet
on the ground.

Swish swish
I make a wish.
Lie on the magic carpet,
fly to the gold palace.
Swim in the
sea of leaves.
Swish swish swish
as quiet as a fish.

Laura Ranger (6)

21st

Sounds

I love to lie and listen
    when I am snug in bed
to whispers of the curtain
    sounds deep in my head

The drop of tap and raindrop
The grown-ups still up late
laughs and barks and footsteps
The snick of garden gate.
I love to hear the clock ticks
The hamster gnawing bars
my mother clicking door locks
The rush of passing cars.
I love to lie and listen
collect the sounds I hear
and every night say,
    "thank you"
for ears that always hear.

Peter Dixon

22nd

Grumpy Bed Said to Jolly Ted

Grumpy Bed said to Ted,
"You're pressing on my head-
      board!"
Jolly Ted said to Bed,
"Sorry, I'll move a bit more
      sideward."
Grumpy Bed said to Ted,
"Isn't that Tom a pest!"
Jolly Ted said to Bed,
"Tom? Little Tom? He's the best!"
Grumpy Bed said to Ted,
"Not when he jumps up and down
      on me!"
Jolly Ted said to Bed,
"He's just a lively boy, silly!"
Grumpy Bed said to Ted,
"He throws my pillows all about!"
Jolly Ted said to Bed,
"It's only when he can't play out!"
Grumpy Bed said to Ted,
"Why can't he keep still like me?"
Jolly Ted said to Bed,
"Because he's too full of energy!"
Grumpy Bed said to Ted,

"It's not much fun being played and
      slept upon!"
Jolly Ted said to Bed,
"It's a job, a good job. Better than
      none!"

Ivan Jones

23rd

Riding On a Giant

I'm riding on a giant.
I'm way up in the sky,
Looking down on everyone
From higher up than high.

I'm holding tight to giant's ears
as we stride along the street
shouting down at people,
Hey! mind my giant's feet!

We're ducking down through
   doorways.
We're walking over walls.
I'm safe as houses way up here –
My giant never falls.

People down below us
Simply stop and stare.
Then when they see our shadow,
Oh wow! They get a scare.

I'm taller than the tree-tops,
I'm high enough to fly.
Another centimetre and I'd
Bump into the sky.

I've been riding on my giant,
Oh! what a day I've had.
I'm not afraid of giants,

'Cos this giant is my dad.

David Whitehead

24th

Skylight

Sleeping in the attic
with a skylight overhead,
you can watch
the moving stars
when you lie in bed:
splintering the darkness,
points of silver light
make their shining journeys
through the deep, far night.

Sometimes, when it's stormy,
you can hear the rain
beating fists
of water on
the cold, bare pane.
Best of all, and loveliest –
like a lost balloon
floating high
above you ... comes
the bright, white moon.

Jean Kenward

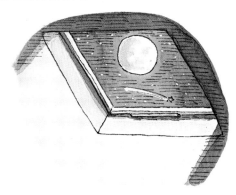

25th

Penalty Shootout

It's a penalty shootout.
If I can save this
The World Cup is ours:
Joy! Happiness! Bliss!
My legs are all wobbly,
My arms are like jelly...
Think of the millions
Watching on telly.
The crowd has gone silent.
The ref walks up slowly.
You could hear a pin drop.
Wish I wasn't a goalie.
The taker's quite nervous –
Tying up his left boot.
He's running up now,
He's going to shoot...
Which way shall I dive?
To left or to right...?

Yipee! I saved it!...

And broke my bedside light!

Eric Finney

26th

If You Were

If you were a sleepy,
Velvety mole,
You'd curl yourself up
In an underground hole.

If you were a wallaby
Baby, I vouch
You'd be tucked up at night
In your mother's warm pouch.

In the tropical forest
The young chimpanzees
Cling tight to their mums
Fast asleep in the trees.

If you slept like a tortoise
The whole winter through,
You'd miss all of Christmas
And New Year's Day, too.

So I think you'll agree,
From all I have said,
That the best place for YOU
Is your warm, comfy bed.

Barry On

27th

Silverly

Silverly,
  Silverly,
Over the
  Trees
The moon drifts
  By on a
Runaway
  Breeze.

Dozily,
  Dozily,
Deep in her
  Bed,
A little girl
  Dreams with the
Moon in her
  Head.

Dennis Lee

209

28th

Anansi and the Moon

Spiderman Anansi
went walking in the night.
Suddenly he noticed
a shining silver light.

He went to have a closer look,
and what was it he found?
A great big shiny silver pearl
lying on the ground.

"Ah!" cried Anansi.
"What a lovely sight!
I'll take it home to give my boys,
and fill them with delight."

But when Anansi showed it,
the boys could not agree.
They all began to argue, saying,
"Give it just to me!"

So, in the end, Anansi
threw it far and high.
It settled there among the stars,
floating in the sky.

And if you look at night-time
you'll see it hanging there:
a lovely round and silver moon
for all of us to share.

Tony Mitton

29th

Hibernating Hedgehog

Here comes Winter,
cold and grey.
It's time to tuck
myself away.

Here comes ice
and here comes snow.
I need somewhere
warm to go.

Here comes mist
and freezing fog.
Here's a good old
hollow log.

And here's a pile
of leaves that's deep.
I'll roll up here
and go to sleep.

Tony Mitton

30th

The Land of Story-Books

At evening when the lamp is lit,
Around the fire my parents sit;
They sit at home and talk and sing,
And do not play at anything.

Now, with my little gun, I crawl
All in the dark along the wall,
And follow round the forest track
Away behind the sofa back.

There, in the night, where none
   can spy,
All in my hunter's camp I lie,
And play at books that I have read
Till it is time to go to bed.

These are the hills, these are the
   woods,
These are my starry solitudes;
And there the river by whose brink
The roaring lion comes to drink.

I see the others far away
As if in firelit camp they lay,
And I, like to an Indian scout,
Around their party prowled about.

So, when my nurse comes in for
   me,
Home I return across the sea,
And go to bed with backward looks
At my dear land of Story-books.

Robert Louis Stevenson

31st

Hallowe'en

Witchy Kittens

The witch's cat had kittens
One dark and spooky night.
A night as black as beetles' backs
With never a chink of light.

She washed them and she fed them
And kept them close and warm
She stayed awake the long, long
     night
To see they took no harm.

She coddled them and cuddled
     them
And licked them clean and dry
She gave them little sips of milk
To still their mewing cry.

Although she could not see a thing
'Twas as black as witches' hats
She counted seven tiny tails
On seven tiny cats.

"I must name my seven babies –
Names all dark and witchy –
I'll call them Ebony, Midnight,
     Inky, Jet,
Licquorice, Charcoal and Pitchy."

Then when she'd named her family
She purred and slept till light
At crack of dawn she woke to find
HER SEVEN BLACK BABES
     WERE WHITE.

David Whitehead

NOVEMBER
1st – 30th

Westward, westward Hiawatha

Sailed into the fiery sunset...

1st

2nd

The Sleeping Giant

The Sleeping Giant
Has been asleep so long,
His body seems part of the land.
He is a hill
On which people stand.
His beard is a forest
In which people play,
Birds nest, tramps stay.
His nostrils are caves
Which people explore.

Is it only me
Who hears him snore
On stormy nights?
Only me who sees
Giant whiskers twitch?
Do other people sleep too tight?

Is it only me
Who hears his giant belly
Grumble and boom?
Only me who feels
His warm breath
Drifting through the windows
Of my room?

Ivan Jones

Star Night

It's the first clear night of winter –
a night as clear as polished glass.
My dad fetches the telescope from
   the attic
where it lives next to old books
and bags full of old clothes.

The telescope stands to attention
on its three spindly legs in the
   garden.
"Oooohhhh!" says my dad, peering
   into it.
"Look!" he tells me.

I look but I can only see the roof.

"Close one eye. No, the other one."
I close one eye ... and suddenly
   STARS!!!
A round field of dancing stars!
Just as if someone had sprinkled
   salt
on black, black paper.

John Rice

214

3rd

Two Little Kittens

Two little kittens, one stormy
   night,
Began to quarrel, and then to fight;
One had a mouse, the other had
   none,
And that's the way the quarrel
   begun.

"I'll have that mouse," said the
   biggest cat;
"You'll have that mouse? We'll see
   about that!"
"I *will* have that mouse," said the
   eldest son;
"You *shan't* have the mouse," said
   the little one.

I told you before 'twas a stormy
   night;
When these two little kittens
   began to fight;
The old woman seized her
   sweeping broom,
And swept the two kittens right
   out of the room.

The ground was covered with frost
   and snow,
And the two little kittens had
   nowhere to go;
So they laid them down on the mat
   at the door,
While the old woman finished
   sweeping the floor.

Then they crept in, as quiet as
   mice,
All wet with the snow, and as cold
   as ice,
For they found it was better, that
   stormy night,
To lie down and sleep than to
   quarrel and fight.

Jane Taylor

4th

Sampan

Waves lap lap
Fish fins clap clap
Brown sails flap flap
Chop-sticks tap tap
Up and down the long green river
Ohe Ohe lanterns quiver
Willow branches brush the river
Ohe Ohe lanterns quiver
Waves lap lap
Fish fins clap clap
Brown sails flap flap
Chop-sticks tap tap

Tao Lang Pee

5th

Bonfire Night

Out of doors at night,
Newspapers piled in our arms,
Scudding in Wellington boots
Through the wet grass of the lawns.

Our misted breath, speech bubbled
As we shove paper in the heap.
Mum and Dad come out laughing
High pitched and belly deep.

Flashlights in the darkness,
White paper's edge and matches.
"Stand back!" Dad calls
As the first spark catches.

Soon the flames of yellow and red
Are licking fierce and high;
Like a dragon's tongue
They flicker into the jet black sky.

Suddenly, B A N G!!
Wheesh! wheesh!
Voices cry: Ooh!! Aah!!
Rockets screeeech!

The fire fades; cheeks glow,
Grown-ups dash for damson wine,
We go for hot sausages and spuds.
No one mentions bedtime.

Ivan Jones

6th

7th

A Proud Old Man (Grandpa)

They say they are healthier
 than me,
Though they can't walk to the
 end of a mile.
At their age I walked forty at night
 to wage battle at dawn.
They think they are healthier
 than me.
If their socks get wet they
 catch cold,
When my sockless feet got wet,
 I never sneezed,
But they still think that they are
 healthier than me.
On a soft mattress over a spring
 bed
They still have to take a sleeping
 pill.
But I, with reeds cutting into my
 ribs
My head resting on a piece of
 wood,
I sleep like a baby and snore.

Paul Chidyausiku

Polar Bear

Polar bear, polar bear,
How do you keep clean?
You always seem to stay so white
No matter where you've been.

My mummy scrubs me every night
To wash the dirt away.
Somehow it all comes back again
When I go out to play.

Polar bear, polar bear,
Do you ever bath?
I seem to get so dirty
Just walking up the path.

I wish I was a polar bear,
So then every night
If someone tries to bath me
I'd growl at them and bite!

Spike Milligan

217

8th

The Moon

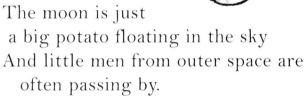

The moon is just
 a big potato floating in the sky
And little men from outer space are
   often passing by.
If they're feeling hungry they eat
   just a bit for dinner,
That's why the moon is sometimes
   fat,
but at other times it's thinner.

Kjartan Poskitt

9th

"Haiku" Friendship Poem

Two boys by firelight
One black face the other white,
Friends in the cold night.

James Stevens (11)

10th

Winter Morning:
Winter Night

This morning I walked to school
through the dark
it was so cold my shadow shivered
under the street lamps.

My feet cracked the ice
that glittered as hard as the frosted
   stars
stuck on the sky's blue back.

Cars crept by like giant cats
their bright eyes shining.

Tonight I walked over the snow
the moon's cool searchlight
splashed its glow over the garden.

Picking out details of rooftops and
   hedges
as clearly and sharply
as a summer stillness just after
   dawn.

Cars on the street roared like lions
bounding over the wet tarmac.

David Harmer

12th

Of Evening in the Wintertime

Of evening in the Wintertime
I hear the cows go home
mooing and lowing by the window
in the muddy loam.

In other places other children
look up and find no stars:
they see tall walls and only hear
buses and motor cars.

I love the muddy lane that lies
beside our lonely house.
In bed I hear all that goes by –
even the smallest mouse.

George Barker

11th

Man in the Moon

Does the Man in the Moon make
   music
as he sits up there alone
as bright as silver paper
and smooth as a pumice stone?

Does he sing to himself, as he
   travels
the great, wide, star-pricked sky?
Or whistle a tune like a blackbird
as he goes sailing by?

Does the Man in the Moon feel
   lonely,
or does he like to be there –
as pale as milk in the morning,
and gold, in the cold night air?

Jean Kenward

13th

Bedtime

Five minutes, five minutes more,
   please!
   Let me stay five minutes more!
Can't I just finish the castle
   I'm building here on the floor?
Can't I just finish the story
   I'm reading here in my book?
Can't I just finish this bead-chain –
   It *almost* is finished, look!
Can't I just finish this game,
   please?
   When a game's once begun
It's a pity never to find out
   Whether you've lost or won.
Can't I just stay five minutes?
   Well, can't I stay just four?
Three minutes, then? two
   minutes?
   Can't I stay *one* minute more?

Eleanor Farjeon

14th

Divali! Divali!

Divali! Divali!
Light the lamps right now!

Let the flames so small and bright
guide us through the darkest night.
Let the flames so small and bright
lead us safely to the light.

Divali! Divali!
Light the lamps right now!

Wes Magee

15th

Naughty Soap Song

Just when I'm ready to
Start on my ears,
That is the time that my
Soap disappears.

It jumps from my fingers and
Slithers and slides
Down to the end of the
Tub, where it hides.

And acts in a most diso-
Bedient way
AND THAT'S WHY MY SOAP'S
  GROWING
THINNER EACH DAY.

Dorothy Aldis

16th

All Through the Night

Sleep, my child, and peace attend
  thee
All through the night.
Guardian angels God will send
  thee
All through the night.
Soft the drowsy hours are creeping,
Hill and vale in slumber sleeping,
I my loving vigil keeping
All through the night.

While the moon her watch is
  keeping
All through the night;
While the weary world is sleeping
All through the night;
O'er thy spirit gently stealing,
Visions of delight revealing,
Breathes a pure and holy feeling
All through the night.

Sir Harold Boulton

My Shadow

I have a little shadow that goes in
   and out with me,
And what can be the use of him is
   more than I can see.
He is very, very like me from the
   heels up to the head;
And I see him jump before me,
   when I jump into my bed.

The funniest thing about him is the
   way he likes to grow –
Not at all like proper children,
   which is always very slow;
For he sometimes shoots up taller
   like an india-rubber ball,
And he sometimes gets so little
   that there's none of him at all.

He hasn't got a notion of how
   children ought to play,
And can only make a fool of me in
   every sort of way.
He stays so close beside me, he's a
   coward you can see;
I'd think shame to stick to nursie
   as that shadow sticks to me!

One morning, very early, before the
   sun was up,
I rose and found the shining dew
   on every buttercup;
But my lazy little shadow, like an
   arrant sleepy-head,
Had stayed at home behind me and
   was fast asleep in bed.

Robert Louis Stevenson

Listening in Bed

If I listen hard
in bed at night,

I can hear
the floor creak,
the door squeak,
the tap leak.

I can hear
the dishes clink
down in the kitchen sink.

I can hear
the telly boom
down in the
    sitting room.

And very near
I can hear
my little brother
breathing deep.
Ssssh...
He's fast asleep.

Tony Mitton

18th

Josie Won't Go Up to Bed

Josie won't go up to bed –
The sheets feel hot,
The pillow hurts her head,
The room's too dark,
The mattress isn't right,
The bed's too small,
The night-light glows too bright,
The floorboards creak,
The ceiling's far too high,
The door won't shut,
Her throat is feeling dry...
And all because
(She thinks we do not know!)
She wants to watch
A Late Night TV Show!

Trevor Harvey

20th

Sleep Potion

Cream from a cow
who's jumped over the moon,
moondust from a silver spoon,
water from an underground stream
and the remains from last night's
   dream:
mix them all together
with an owl's feather
and then bake it well at midnight
until it's crispy and light.
When cool, crumble it as fine as
   dust,
sprinkle over your child
and fall to sleep they must.

Tim Pointon

21st

Early to Bed

Is it nearly bedtime yet?
I stretch and rub my eyes,
I think I'd like to go up now,
No reason for surprise.

I know I like to stay up late
More often than is right.
But just this once, if you don't
   mind,
I'd like an early night.

It doesn't mean I'm feeling ill,
I *could* stay up a while.
But I'd much sooner go to bed,
I don't know why you smile.

So now I think I'll say goodnight,
(I really can't stop yawning)
And oh, I've just remembered, it's
My birthday in the morning.

Barry On

22nd

23rd

Thanksgiving

A City Ditty

Thank You
  for all my hands can hold –
    apples red,
    and melons gold,
    yellow corn
      both ripe and sweet,
      peas and beans
        so good to eat!

Thank You
  for all my eyes can see –
    lovely sunlight,
    field and tree,
    white cloud-boats
      in sea-deep sky,
      soaring bird
        and butterfly.

Thank You
  for all my ears can hear –
    birds' song echoing
    far and near,
    songs of little
      stream, big sea,
      cricket, bullfrog,
        duck and bee!

Ivy O. Eastwick

Blackout in the buildings,
the big fuse blew;
no electric current,
what will we do?

Can't use the telephone,
can't make toast,
can't use the stereo,
boo, you're a ghost.

Frozen juice cans
getting runny,
frozen meat is
smelling funny.

Traffic signals out
and headlights on the cars,
but what do you know?
We can see the moon and stars.

Eve Merriam

24th

A Night With a Wolf

High up on the lonely mountains,
   Where the wild men watched and
      waited;
Wolves in the forest, and bears in
   the bush,
   And I on my path belated.

The rain and the night together
   Came down, and the wind came
      after,
Bending the props of the pine-tree
   roof,
   And snapping many a rafter.

I crept along in the darkness,
   Stunned, and bruised, and
      blinded;
Crept to a fir with thick-set
   boughs,
   And a sheltering rock behind it.

There, from the blowing and
   raining,
   Crouching, I sought to hide me.
Something rustled; two green eyes
   shone;
   And a wolf lay down beside me!

His wet fur pressed against me;
   Each of us warmed the other;
Each of us felt, in the stormy dark,
   That beast and man were
      brother.

And when the falling forest
   No longer crashed in warning,
Each of us went from our hiding
   place
   Forth in the wild, wet morning.

Bayard Taylor

25th

Midnight Snow

One night as I lay sleeping
And dreams ran through my head
The night breeze stirred my
 curtain
And moonlight bathed my bed.
I walked up to the window
And leaned upon the ledge
Saw drifting snowflakes falling
On road and land and hedge.

Midnight snow
Drifting snow
While the world lies sleeping
And only me, here to see
Those snowflakes gently falling.

And all along the roadway
The blanket lies unstirred
No tracks of tyres or sledges
No print of fox or bird.
No footsteps in the garden
No sound upon the air
A million petals falling
Silent as a prayer.

Midnight snow
Drifting snow
While the world lies sleeping
And only me, here to see
Those snowflakes gently falling.

Gareth Owen
Taken from the Welsh hymn: Y Milur
Bychan *by Joseph Parry*

26th

The Bedroom-Messer Monster

I've got a big box where I'm meant
    to put
My toys to keep them neat.
Mum doesn't like having trucks
    and trains
And teddy bears under her feet.
But one thing Mum can't
    understand
Is that deep inside the crate,
The stripy Bedroom-Messer
    Monster
Quietly lies in wait.

It sleeps very snugly deep in its
    box,
As quiet as a mouse all day,
But when it feels toys pile up on its
    back
It stretches and starts to play.
It jiggles and wriggles and giggles
    and grins,
And bounces a ball on its nose,
And juggles a dozen soft toys in
    the air
With its tail and fingers and toes.

It wiggles its bottom and wags its
    tail
And puffs out its tummy so
That the box is full of its stripy
    shape,
And the toys have nowhere to go.
So I have to hope that Mum forgets
That I said I'd clear my room,
And hope my messy and monstrous
    friend
Will sleep again quite soon.

Julia Rawlinson

27th

My Moons

I love my clipped finger-nail moon
A sliver of silver
In a black backdrop sky
A gently rocking sailboat
Bobbing behind the swift night
  clouds.

Another moon I see
Is like a once-bitten iced bun
High over the night chimneys
Waiting for the dawn birds
To peck it away.

My strangest is the daylight moon
Lost in space
Longing for the night-time
Pale-faced, sad
Bleached by the sun.

I love my many moons
But, best of all
Is my bedtime moon
Huge and whole
A round white smiling kite
With a tail of silver stars.

David Whitehead

28th

Granny

It so nice to have a Granny
when you've had it from yuh
  Mammy
and you feeling down and dammy

It so nice to have a Granny
when she brings you bread and
  jammy
and says, "Tell it all to Granny."

Grace Nichols

30th

from **Hiawatha**

On the shore stood Hiawatha,
Turned and waved his hand at
   parting;
On the clear and luminous water
Launched his birch-canoe for
   sailing,
From the pebbles of the margin
Shoved it forth into the water;
Whispered to it: "Westward!
   Westward!"
And with speed it darted forward.
And the evening sun descending
Set the clouds on fire with redness,
Burned the broad sky, like a prairie,
Left upon the level water
One long track and trail of
   splendour,
Down whose stream, as down a
   river,
Westward, westward Hiawatha
Sailed into the fiery sunset,
Sailed into the purple vapours,
Sailed into the dusk of evening.

Henry Wadsworth Longfellow

29th

Who Am I?

I am the oldest of the bears
but I will never die!
I wander slowly, silently
beneath the midnight sky.

I am the largest of the bears;
I cannot sleep or fly,
and yet I rest above the clouds
and dance when the moon is high.

I am the farthest of the bears;
beyond the sun I lie!
I wander with a million stars...

I'm the Great Bear in the sky!

Judith Nicholls

DECEMBER
1st – 31st

Santa Claws has snowy whiskers,

fur of ginger-red...

DECEMBER
1st

1st

from **Night Mail**

This is the Night Mail crossing the
  border,
Bringing the cheque and the postal
  order,

Letters for the rich, letters for the
  poor,
The shop at the corner, the girl
  next door.

Pulling up Beattock, a steady
  climb:
The gradient's against her, but
  she's on time.

Past cotton-grass and moorland
  boulder,
Shovelling white steam over her
  shoulder,

Snorting noisily, she passes
Silent miles of wind-bent grasses.

Birds turn their heads as she
  approaches,
Stare from bushes at her blank-
  faced coaches.

Sheep-dogs cannot turn her course;
They slumber on with paws across.

In the farm she passes no one
  wakes,
But a jug in a bedroom gently
  shakes.

W.H. Auden

2nd

Moon Song

Some like flying on a carpet.
Some like going by balloon.
But I like floating up through space
to swing on the silver moon.

Some like lying on a lazy cloud
to listen to the wind's soft tune.
But I like floating up through space
to swing on the silver moon.

Some like riding on a rocket.
It's ready and leaving soon.
But I like floating up through space
to swing on the silver moon.

*Yes, I like floating up through space
to swing on the silver moon.*

Tony Mitton

3rd

Somersaults

It's fun turning somersaults
and bouncing on the bed,
I walk on my hands
and I stand on my head.

I swing like a monkey
and I tumble and I shake,
I stretch and I bend,
but I never, never break.

I wiggle like a worm
and I wriggle like an eel,
I hop like a rabbit
and I flop like a seal.

I leap like a frog
and I jump like a flea,
there must be a rubber
inside of me.

Jack Prelutsky

4th

Purring

When my cat sleeps
   Curled up in a ball,
You can't really see
   Her head at all.

A furry circle,
   Curled around,
Sleeping softly
   With a purring sound.

She looks funny,
   Does our cat,
Like a furry,
   Purring hat.

I'd like to wear her
   On my head,
Or have her warm
   My toes in bed.

And when you touch her,
   Curled and warm,
Her purring purrs
   All up your arm.

But then she hears
   A sudden sound
And she's no longer
   Curled around;

She's not sleeping,
   Softly there.
She's gone – but left
   Some purring air.

Tony Bradman

5th

Scarlet Ribbons

I peeked in to say Good night
And then I heard my child in prayer,
"And for me some scarlet ribbons,
Scarlet ribbons for my hair."

All the stores were closed and
    shuttered,
All the streets were dark and bare,
In our town no scarlet ribbons,
Not one ribbon for her hair.

Through the night my heart was
    aching,
Just before the dawn was breaking,

I peeked in and on her bed
In gay profusion lying there,
Lovely ribbons, scarlet ribbons,
Scarlet ribbons for her hair.

If I live to be two hundred,
I will never know from where,
Came those lovely scarlet ribbons,
Scarlet ribbons for her hair.

Evelyn Danzig

6th

Burundi Lullaby

A heart to hate you
Is as far away as the moon.
A heart to love you
Is as close as the door.

Anon

7th

Winter

When icicles hang by the wall
  And Dick the shepherd blows his
    nail,
And Tom bears logs into the hall,
  And milk comes frozen home in
    pail;
When blood is nipt, and ways be
    foul,
Then nightly sings the staring owl
      Tuwhoo!
Tuwhit! tuwhoo! A merry note!
While greasy Joan doth keel the
  pot.

When all around the wind doth
  blow,
  And coughing drowns the
    parson's saw,
And birds sit brooding in the snow,
  And Marian's nose looks red and
    raw;
When roasted crabs hiss in the
  bowl
Then nightly sings the staring owl
      Tuwhoo!
Tuwhit! tuwhoo! A merry note!
While greasy Joan doth keel the pot.

William Shakespeare

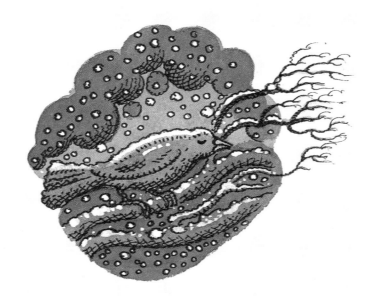

8th

The Blanket of Dreams

I've got a secret. I'll whisper it:
I still go to bed with a little bit
Of blanket I've had since I was born.
It's tattered now, all old and torn.
But this blanket isn't what it seems,
It's really useful – in my dreams.
It gets me out of lots of jams –
When, in a dream, I've just been
    rammed
By pirate ships and left to float
On the wild, wild sea in a tiny boat
And packs of sharks come sniffing
    by
With toothy grins and eager eyes
And lightning cracks and my
    engines fail,
My blanket makes a brilliant sail!
I simply hoist it up the mast:
"Get me out this nightmare FAST!"
Or when I dream that I've got lost
In Arctic wastes of ice and frost
Among icebergs that glitter blue
Where shivering coldness chills me
    through,
Then I wrap my blanket round me
    tight
And it keeps me cosy through the
    night
Until I come back with the dawn

Into my own bed, safe and warm.
Mum says: "Put that blanket in the
    bin!
It looks like something the cat's
    brought in!"
But she doesn't know the things
    it's been –
 a magic carpet, a trampoline,
A cloak of invisibility!
What adventures we've had, my
    blanket and me
And what amazing sights we've
    seen,
Travelling together through my
    dreams.

Susan Gates

9th

Home at Last

We struggled round shops in cold,
    rainy weather,
My mum and my brother and me
    together;
Then when we got home, we found
    that our dad
Had made up a fire – oh, weren't
    we glad!

I wriggled at bathtime right out of
    my clothes,
And dad put some cream on my
    poor, sore nose.
The water was hot, but I still felt
    freezing;
While mum got me dry, I couldn't
    stop sneezing.

I duggled down close and cuddled
    my mum,
She read me a story and I sucked
    my thumb;
Outside our house the wind howled
    round,
And I could hear rain splashing
    down on the ground.

I snuggled and duggled, deep down
    in my bed,
I pulled all the covers right over
    my head;
Outside I could hear the wild,
    roaring storm,
But there in my bed it was all nice
    and warm.

Tony Bradman

10th

The Traveller

Old man, old man, sitting on the
    stile,
Your boots are worn, your clothes
    are torn,
        Tell us why you smile.

Children, children, what silly
    things you are!
My boots are worn and my clothes
    are torn
        Because I've walked so far.

Old man, old man, where have you
    walked from?
Your legs are bent, your breath is
    spent –
        Which way did you come?

Children, children, when you're old
    and lame,
When your legs are bent and your
    breath is spent
        You'll know the way I came.

Old man, old man, have you far
    to go
Without a friend to your journey's
    end,
        And why are you so slow?

Children, children, I do the best
    I may:
I meet a friend at my journey's end
        With whom you'll meet some
        day.

Old man, old man, sitting on the
    stile,
How do you know which way to go,
        And why is it you smile?

Children, children, butter should
    be spread,
Floors should be swept and
    promises kept –
        And you should be in bed!

Raymond Wilson

11th

Listen

Shhhhhhhhhhhhhhhhhhhhhhhhhhhh!
Sit still, very still
And listen.
Listen to wings
Lighter than eyelashes
Stroking the air.
Know what the thin breeze
Whispers on high
To the coconut trees.
Listen and hear.

Telcine Turner

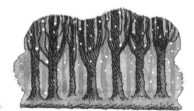

12th

Stopping By Woods on a Snowy Evening

Whose woods these are I think I
   know.
His house is in the village though;
He will not see me stopping here
To watch his woods fill up with
   snow.

My little horse must think it queer
To stop without a farmhouse near
Between the woods and frozen lake
The darkest evening of the year.

He gives his harness bells a shake
To ask if there is some mistake.
The only other sound's the sweep
Of easy wind and downy flake.

The woods are lovely, dark and
   deep,
But I have promises to keep,
And miles to go before I sleep,
And miles to go before I sleep.

Robert Frost

13th

Festival of St Lucia

Crown of Light Festival

Stars gleaming overhead,
    evening air's clear,
    and Advent is here,
    now in Sweden.
Golden-haired girls
    in each village and town
    wear a white flowing gown,
    now in Sweden.
With a crown of green leaves,
    and candles all bright,
    on St Lucia's night,
    now in Sweden.
Snowflakes are dancing,
    as bells start to ring,
    and the children's choirs
    sing,
    now in Sweden.

David Bateson

14th

Sloth Song

I wish I were a sloth
And lived life upside down,
The sky below, the ground above,
In the jungle instead of the town.

I wish I were a sloth,
Just a bundle of shaggy hair,
I'd never have to budge an inch,
'Cos nobody'd know I was there.

I wish I were a sloth,
So I could sleep all day,
Curled up in a cosy ball,
I'd dream my life away.

Dilys Rose

15th

In My Bath

In my bath is
a rubber duck
a bear with one ear
a bit of muck
wooden lorries
a plastic frog
a blob of soap
a woolly dog
my dinner dish
some odd red stuff
a bobbing boat
a ball of fluff
a piece of cheese
a soggy pea
a lot of water
a lot of water
and
me.

Dave Calder

16th

Animal Tired

You are dog tired, little one –
Mr Sleep has finally won.
You need more than a catnap now –
even if that yawn sounded like a
    meow.
Let's tuck you in like a bunny in a
    burrow –
now you're yawning like a hippo.
It's time for a beautiful whale of a
    dream –
not one the size of a stickleback in
    a stream.
It's time for a real elephant of a
    sleep –
now close those eyes and don't
    peep.

Tim Pointon

17th

Lullaby

I'll sing you a song of the stars of
   the night
And the white moon over the sea;
I'll sing you a song of the wide-
   eyed child,
Who's awake and watching me.

I'll sing you a song of the birds of
   the air,
Cry of curlew and eagle swoop;
I'll sing you a song of the drowsy
   child,
Whose eyelids begin to droop.

I'll sing you a song of the hump-
   back whale,
The tiger, the lamb and the bear;
I'll sing you a song of the sleepy
   child,
Who is nearly, nearly there.

I'll sing you a song of the
   mountains and hills,
The forests and oceans so deep;
I'll sing you a song of the
   dreaming child,
Who at last has fallen asleep.

Barry On

18th

Half Moon Cottage

Half Moon Cottage –
A sliver of a place –
Was there this morning,
Tonight it's just a space!

Half Moon Cottage
One room wide
Whispered "Hold tight!" to the
   furniture
And took it for a ride.

Sue Cowling

DECEMBER
19th

19th

The Lighthouse

When I am in my bed at night
And whispers fill the darkened hall,
The friendly lighthouse on the
   island
Flashes on my bedroom wall.

Flash! there's Teddy on the chair,
Flash! my empty mug and plate,
Flash! my clock and dressing gown –
Then darkness till I count to eight.

In summer when the sea is silver
And the moon is flying high,
I think of sailors keeping watch
Upon the steamers passing by.

But when the sea is blind with fog
The lighthouse siren gives a roar,
Then I dream of lonely monsters
Rising from the ocean floor.

Winter storms beat on my window
And the sea is wild with foam,
Then the lighthouse guards my
   sleep
And guides the sailors safely home.

Alan Temperley

20th

Reindeer

Far, far away
the reindeer live
in a land of ice
and snow...

When it's nearly
Christmas,
I wonder if
they know?

Nuzzling around
for a nibble of moss
in the freezing, arctic
day –

Do they guess
there's a sledge to pull
miles and miles
away?

Under a wide
star-sprinkled sky
that's shining
winter-bright,

Father Christmas
is loading up...
ready for
Christmas night!

Jean Kenward

21st

This is the Hand

This is the hand
that touched the frost
that froze my tongue
and made it numb

this is the hand
that cracked the nut
that went in my mouth
and never came out

this is the hand
that slid round the bath
to find the soap
that wouldn't float

this is the hand
on the hot water bottle
meant to warm my bed
that got lost instead

this is the hand
that held the bottle
that let go of the soap
that cracked the nut
that touched the frost
this is the hand
that never gets lost.

Michael Rosen

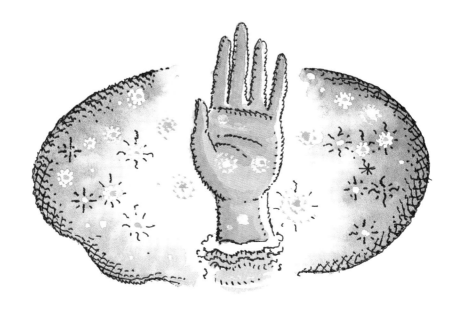

22nd

The Snowman

Mother, while you were at the
   shops
and I was snoozing in my chair
I heard a tap at the window
saw a snowman standing there

He looked so cold and miserable
I almost could have cried
so I put the kettle on
and invited him inside

I made him a cup of cocoa
to warm the cockles of his nose
then he snuggled in front of the
   fire
for a cosy little doze

He lay there warm and smiling
softly counting sheep
I eavesdropped for a little while
then I too fell asleep

Seems he awoke and tiptoed out
exactly when I'm not too sure
it's a wonder you didn't see him
as you came in through the door

(oh, and by the way,
the kitten's made a puddle on the
   floor)

Roger McGough

DECEMBER
23rd & 24th

That Day

I know I'll awake on that morning
Around about six a.m.,
Feel lumps in my Christmas
   stocking
And know that it's here again.

Later on there'll be Christmas
   crackers,
Brazil nuts and dates and figs
And a Christmas tree with an angel
And parcels and sugar pigs.

There's sure to be holly with
   berries
And pearls on the mistletoe,
And frosty ferns on the window
   pane –
Maybe there'll even be snow.

And perhaps on the night of
   Christmas,
In the east – or is it the west?
I'll see millions of stars, but just
   one star
Brighter than all the rest.

Eric Finney

Santa Claws
(or What Mama Puss Told Her
Kittens on Christmas Eve)

Santa Claws has snowy whiskers,
fur of ginger-red.
Santa Claws comes rooftop
   roaming
when you're curled in bed.

Santa Claws will bring you
   presents
if you wait and wish –
a ball of wool, a sugar mouse,
purrhaps a shining fish.

Santa gets his paws all sooty,
scrambling through the hearth.
When he's made his midnight visits
Santa needs a bath!

Santa's sneaking through the
   moonlight,
slinking in his sleigh.
Time to go to sleep now, pussies.
Soon it's *Kitmas Day!*

Tony Mitton

25th

Christmas Day

The Christmas Donkey

I am the donkey who saw it all.
  I saw the couple come –
Joseph and Mary wrapped in a
    shawl –
  And the birth of their tiny son.

I warmed the baby with my hot
    breath
  While the night grew cold and
    sharp.
As He smiled at me from His bed of
    straw
  Light shone round His head in
    the dark.

And a stream of visitors came to
    my stable
  Guided by a bright star
And angels who sang of peace to
    all people
  Wherever, whoever, they are.

But the animals were not forgotten;
  Blessed and happy were we
To be first at the birth of the Holy
    Child
  And to stay with His family.

I am the donkey who saw it all –
  I saw the shepherds come
And three Wise Men, with their
    gifts of gold
  For the baby born in my home.

Mal Lewis Jones

26th

Boxing Day

A Star to Guide You

Before you go to bed
Put on your boots
Hold my hand
And come outside

See the stars?
Each one has got a name
I know because I put them there

Before I was born
Before the wise men came
Before the shepherds brought a
    lamb
I sung for you
And made a universe

Look south and up
See Orion the Mighty Hunter?
From his belt go right
Find the brightest star
That's for you

Reach up, hold tight
And call its name out loud
Pull down a silver twinkling thread
And tie it round your wrist

Back to bed, the thread won't break
Dream silver starlit dreams
And everyday for evermore
Your star will guide you to me

Brice Avery

27th

Christmas Thank Yous

Dear Auntie
Oh, what a nice jumper
I've always adored powder blue
and fancy you thinking of
orange and pink
for the stripes
how clever of you!

Dear Uncle
The soap is
terrific
So useful
and such a kind
thought and
how did you guess that
I'd just used the last of
the soap that last Christmas
brought

Dear Gran
Many thanks for the hankies
Now I really can't wait for the flu
and the daisies embroidered
in red round the "M"
for Michael
how
thoughtful of you!

Dear Cousin
What socks!
and the same sort you wear
so you must be
the last word in style
and I'm certain you're right that
the luminous green
will make me stand out a mile

Dear Sister
I quite understand your concern
it's a risk sending jam in the post
But I think I've pulled out
all the big bits
of glass
so it won't taste too
sharp spread on toast

Dear Grandad
Don't fret
I'm delighted
So *don't* think your gift will
offend
I'm not at all hurt
that you gave up this year
and just sent me
a fiver
to spend

Mick Gowar

28th

Snug

Let's close the curtains on the
   night:
It looks like snow.
Let's just sit here in the firelight,
Its shadow show.

Let's bring our tea in by the telly.
There's cherry cake,
Hot buttered toast, ice cream and
   jelly:
A feast we'll make.

Build up the fire and make sparks
   fly,
Fill up your mug.
The snow tomorrow may be
   mountains high:
Tonight we're snug.

Eric Finney

29th

Christmas Star

I am the star
that squints in the sky.

I am the sky
that squats on the cloud.

I am the cloud
that squirts the earth.

I am the earth
that squeezes the worm.

I am the worm
that squirms under the bird.

I am the bird
that squawks at the cloud.

I am the cloud
that squelches in the sky.

I am the sky
that squabbles with stars.

I am the star
that squints in the sky.

John Rice

30th

The Land of Nod

From breakfast on through all the
      day
At home among my friends I stay;
But every night I go abroad
Afar into the land of Nod.

All by myself I have to go,
With none to tell me what to do –
All alone beside the streams
And up the mountain-sides of
      dreams.

The strangest things are there for
      me,
Both things to eat and things to see,
And many frightening sights
      abroad
Till morning in the land of Nod.

Try as I like to find the way,
I never can get back by day,
Nor can remember plain and clear
The curious music that I hear.

Robert Louis Stevenson

31st

New Year's Eve

The Best Year I've Ever Had

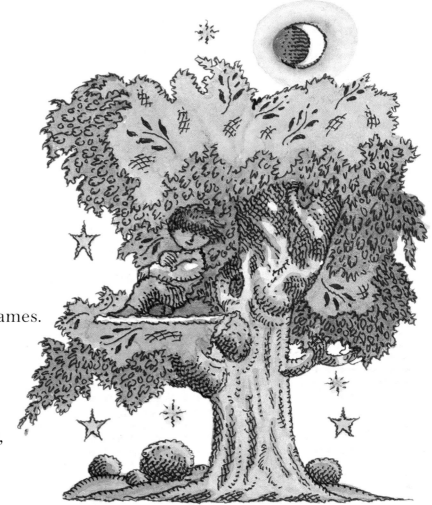

Goodnight, Mum,
Goodnight, Dad.
That was the best year
I've ever had.
I learned such a lot –
How to swim,
How to skate,
Made some new friends,
Found out how to bake.
Watched lots of football,
Played lots of games,
Saw some great films
With strange sounding names.
Made a tree house,
Had a picnic with Clare.
Now it's all over,
I'm tired as old Bear
So read me a poem please,
The last one I'll hear...
But tomorrow, tomorrow,
We start a new year!

Ivan Jones

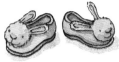  # INDEX

Acknowledgements

The compilers and publishers would like to thank the following for permission to use copyright material in this collection. The publishers have made every effort to contact the copyright holders but there are a few cases where it has not been possible to do so. We would be grateful to hear from anyone who can enable us to contact them so that the omission can be corrected at the first opportunity.

Anne Adeney for "Boring Old Bed" and "Fourth of July" – By kind permission of John Agard c/o Caroline Sheldon Literary Agency for "Bedbugs Marching Song" from *We Animals Would Like a Word With You*, pub. Red Fox (1996) – Dorothy Aldis for "Naughty Soap Song", from *All Together*, pub. Penguin Putnam Inc – W.H. Auden for "Night Mail" from *Collected Poems*, reprinted by permission of Faber & Faber Ltd and Random House, Inc. – Brice Avery for "A Star to Guide You" – Leo Aylen for "Greedy Green River" – Marjorie Baker for "Jerboa" – Kevin Bamford for "I Wear a Daffodil on David's Day" – Elspeth Barker for "Of Evening in the Wintertime" by George Barker – Carey Blyton for "Bananas" and "The Plug Hole Man" – Tony Bradman for "All Night" from *A Kiss On the Nose*, pub. Heinemann. Reproduced by permission of The Agency London Ltd and "Purring" and "Home at Last" from *Smile Please*, pub. Viking Kestrel – David Higham Associates for "The Little Griffin Bird" by Henrietta Branford – Dave Calder for "The Room" and "In My Bath" – Alfonso Caso for "Aztec Song" from *The Aztecs: People of the Sun*, translated by Lowell Dunham, pub. University of Oklahoma Press – Charles Causley for "Charity Chadder" from *Early in the Morning*, pub. Macmillan – Wanda Chotomska for "Hovercrafts" – The Literary Executor of Leonard Clark for "Good Company" – Wendy Cope for "Song of the Big Toe" and "Into the Bathtub" – John Cotton for "Torches at Night" and "Our Cat at Night" – John Coutts for "On the Beach" – Sue Cowling for "Recipe for a Good Night's Sleep", "Night Hunter", "Night in the Jungle", "Quiet Things", "Moony, Moony, Macaroony", "Late Night Caller" and "Half Moon Cottage" – Jennifer Curry for "Moving" – Evelyn Danzig for "Scarlet Ribbons" pub. EMI Mills Music Incl, UsSA and EMI Harmonies Ltd. Worldwide print rights controlled by Warner Bros, Inc, USA/IMP Ltd. Reproduced by permission of IMP Ltd – Mary Dawson-Jeffries for "Snow Lady" from *Twinkle Twinkle Chocolate Bar*, pub. OUP – Walter de la Mare for "The Horseman", "Old Shellover", "Five Eyes" and "I Met at Eve" – Emily Dickinson for "Will There Really Be a Morning?" from *The Poems of Emily Dickinson*, pub. The Belknap Press of Harvard University Press – Peter Dixon for "Sounds" and "Prayers" – Berlie Doherty for "Badger" and "Night Sounds" from *Walking On Air*, pub. HarperCollins – Olive Dove for "Who Spoke" – Malachy Doyle for "The Dancing Tiger" and "St Patrick's Day" – Lauris Edmond for "Apple" from *I'm Glad the Sky is Painted Blue*, pub. Julia MacRae – Richard Edwards for "Littlemouse" and "Badgers" from *The Word Party*, pub. Lutterworth Press – Eleanor Farjeon for "The Night will Never Stay" and "Bedtime" from *Silver Sand and Snow*, pub. Michael Joseph, and "Cats" and "Ned" from *The Children's Bell*s, pub. Oxford University Press (OUP) – Max Fatchen for "Corroboree" – Joshua Feehan for "Sleeping in School" – David Fickling for "The Tiny Little Rocket" – Eric Finney for "My Insect Dream", "That Day", "Snug", "Penalty Shoot-Out", "Thank-You Letter" and "Five Little Puppies" – Pauline Fisk for "White Dog, Black Beach" – Sally Flood for "Holy Day" – John Foster for "Sitting in my Bathtub" from *Twinkle Twinkle Chocolate Bar*, pub. OUP, "What's That?" from *Ghost Poems*, pub. OUP, and "Where Are You Going, Jenny?" from *Doctor Proctor and Other Rhymes*, pub. OUP – The Estate of Robert Frost for "Stopping by Woods on a Snowy Evening" from *The Poetry of Robert Frost*, pub. Jonathan Cape – The Society of Authors as the Literary Representative of the Estate of Rose Fyleman & George H. Doran Co. for *Mrs Brown* and *Fairies* by Rose Fyleman, reproduced by permission of Doubleday, a division of Random House, Inc. – Roger Garfitt for "As the Old Russian Said" – Susan Gates for "Blanket of Dreams" – Adèle Geras for "Nightlight" – Mick Gowar for "Bedtime Riddle" and "Christmas Thank Yous" – David Harmer for "Winter Morning: Winter Night" – Trevor Harvey for "Power Cut" and "Josie Won't Go to Bed" – Jim Hatfield for "When You Close those Tired Eyes", "March Winds", "Bedtime Story", "The Laughing Buddha" and "Miland-an-Nabi" – Adrian Henri for "H25" from *Dinner with the Spratts*, pub. Methuen – Cicely Herbert for "Tell Me Why" and "A Mime of Information" – Mary Ann Hoberman for "The Folk Who Live in Backward Town" from *The Llama Who Had No Pajama*, pub. Harcourt Brace/Browndeer Press. Reprinted by permission of Gina Maccoby Literary Agency & Harcourt, Inc. – Pamela Hodge for "Tom Scare-no-Crow" – Langston Hughes for "April Rain Song" from *Collected Poems*, pub. Alfred A. Knopf Inc – Ted Hughes for "Dog" from *What is the Truth*, pub. Faber & Faber Ltd – Randell Jarrel for "Bats" from *The Bat Poet*, pub. Michael di Capua Books/HarperCollins – Ivan Jones for "Sleep is like Snowflakes", "Teddydums in Bed", "Up the Wooden Hill", "Jemima", "I've Slept Everywhere", "Strawberry Pillows, Ice-cream Sheets", "Ten Tired Tigers", "Grey Cells", "The Wriggly Itches", "What to Take to Bed in Summer", "Birthday Bike", "Milk Boy", "Heaven", "The Sleeping Giant", "Bonfire Night", "Bed Said to Ted", "Noah's Trick" and "The Best Year I've Ever Had" – Jessie Lewis Jones for "Cat on the Rooftop" –Mal Lewis Jones for "Krishna's Friends", "Easter Eggs", "The Maypole", "Christmas Donkey" and adaptations of "Wee Willy Winkie" and "Babes in the Wood" – Mike Jubb for "A Spell for Sleeping" and "Magic in the Moonlight" – Jean Kenward for "Dragon", "Great Bear and Little Bear", "Skylight", "Reindeer" and "Man in the Moon" – Rudyard Kipling for "The White Seal's Lullaby" from *The Definitive Edition of Rudyard Kipling's Verse* – Ted Kooser for "Rooming House", renamed and reprinted by permission of the University of Pittsburgh Press – Dennis Lee for "The Snowstorm" and "Silverly" from *Jelly Belly*, pub. Macmillan of Canada – Pat Leighton for "Babes-in-the-Moon", "Invasion", "Who Believes in Fairies?", "Holiday Dreams", "Dream Catcher" and "Painting the Moon" – Liz Lochhead for "Bat Chant" – Wes Magee for "My List of Promises", "Here You Lie", "Books at Bedtime", "In the Bath", "Sleeping", "The Bestest Bear Song", "My Book of Animals" and "Divali! Divali!" – Margaret Mahy for "Cat in the Dark" © Margaret Mahy (1993) – Carol Ann Martin for "The Night Tree" – The Society of Authors as the Literary Representative of the Estate of John Masefield for "Sea-Fever" – Andrew Matthews for "Dream Horses", "Granny and Broomstick" and "The Waltzing Polar Bears" reprinted by permission of The Peters, Fraser & Dunlop Group Ltd – Marc Matthews for "Friday Night Smell" – Shirley McDermot for "Fred in Bed" – Roger McGough for "I've Taken to My Bed" and "Snuggles" from *Pillow Talk*, pub. Viking/Puffin, "Mrs Moon" from *Sky in the Pie*, pub. Kestrel/Puffin, "Catapillow" from *Another Day on Your Feet and I Would Have Died*, pub. Macmillan and "The Snowman" from *The Kingfisher Book of Comic Verse*, pub. Kingfisher. Reprinted by permission of The Peters, Fraser & Dunlop Group Ltd – Eve Merriam for "A City Ditty" and "Night Light", reproduced by permission of Marian Reiner, NY – Spike Milligan for "Kangaroo – Kangaroo!", "The ABC", "Two Funny Men" and "Polar Bear" – A.A. Milne for "Furry Bear" from *Now We Are Six*, pub. Methuen. Permission for USA/Canada granted by Dutton Children's Books, a division of Penguin Putnam Inc – Tony Mitton for "Santa Claws", "Moon Song", "Listening in Bed", "Hibernating Hedgehog", "Sea Bed", "Sleepy Sheep", "The Squeak", "Up the Stairs to Bedfordshire", "My Bed", "Tooth Fairies", "My Crocodile", "Goodnight Moon", "The Long Horse", "Hairwashing", "The Toys' Playtime", "Babysitter" and "Anansi and the Moon" – John Mole for "A Song at Bedtime" – Pansy Rose Napaljarri for "The Kangaroo" from *Inside Black Australia*, pub. Penguin Australia – Curtis Brown Ltd and Little, Brown & Co. Inc for Ogden Nash's "Sweet Dreams" and "Morning Prayer" – The Estate of bp Nichol for "A Path to the Moon" from *Giants, Moosequakes and Other Disasters*, pub. Black Moss Press – Judith Nicholls for "Dragonbirth" and "Who Am I?" from *Storm's Eye*, pub. OUP – Grace Nichols for "I Like to Stay Up", "Granny Please Comb my Hair" and "Granny" reproduced by permission of Curtis Brown Ltd, – Jenny Nimmo for "Night Bird" – Barry On for "What Can Be Got Out of Bedtime?", "If You Were", "Early to Bed" and 'Lullaby" reproduced by permission of the author c/o Rogers, Coleridge & White Ltd – Gareth Owen for "Moon", "Life as a Sheep", "Before the Beginning", "Bedmobile", "Pearl" and "Midnight Snow" from *My Granny is a Sumo Wrestler*, pub. Young Lions and "This and That" from *Salford Road and Other Poems*, pub. Young Lions and "I Will Not Fall Asleep" – Brian Patten for "Mooning", " 'It's Time for Bed, You Know' ", "Hushabye Lullaby" and "The Whale's Hymn" – Andrew Fusek Peters for "Questions Before Sleep" from *Sheep Don't Go to Schoo*l, pub. Bloodaxe Books, "Just for Fun" and "Hide and Seek" – Penguin Books for "Hare, Mr Hare" from *The Penguin Book of Japanese Verse*, edited and translated by Geoffrey Bownas and Anthony Thwaite, pub. Penguin Books – Sylvia Plath for "The Bed Book" from *The Bed Book*, pub. Faber & Faber Ltd – Tim Pointon for "The Sleep Train", "Sleep Potion" and "Animal Tired" – Kjartan Poskitt for "In the Bath" and "The Moon" – Joan Poulson for "Night" – Jack Prelutsky for "I Wonder Why Dad is So Thoroughly Mad" from *New Kid On the Block*; "Somersaults" and "Last Night I Dreamed of Chickens" from *Something Big Has Been Here*, pub. by Heinemann and reproduced by permission of Egmont Children's Books and HarperCollins Inc. – Laura Ranger for "God", "It Gets Dark" and "Autumn Leaves" with the permission of Random House New Zealand – Julia Rawlinson for "The Bedroom Messer Monster" – Irene Rawnsley for "Night Train" from *Poetry Corner 2*, pub. BBC Worldwide Limited – Malvina Reynolds for "Morningtown Ride" from *Apusskidu, Songs for Children* – John Rice for "Christmas Star" from *Bears Don't Like Bananas*, pub. Simon and Schuster, and "Over the Sky to See", "The Satellite Circus", "Bedtime, Rhymetime", "Midnight's Moon", "Stargrazing", "Sun Dog, Star Bird, Moon Cat" and "Star Night" – Penelope Rieu for "The Happy Hedgehog" by E.V. Rieu – Dilys Rose for "Sloth Song" – Harold Rosen for "Seder Night" – Michael Rosen for "What If?" from *Under the Bed*, © 1986. Illustrated by Quentin Blake. Reproduced by permission of Walker Books Ltd; "Who Likes Cuddles?" from *Don't Put Mustard in the Custard*, "Mum Reads to Me Every Night" from *Who Drew on the Baby's Head?* and "This is the Hand" from *You Can't Catch Me*, all pub. Scholastic – Fred Sedgwick for "Goodnight" and "Once There Was a Unicorn" – Anne Serraillier for "The Mouse in the Wainscot" by Ian Serraillier – Izumi Shikibu for "On Nights When Hail" from *A Book of Women Poets from Antiquity to Now*, pub. Shocken Books, distributed by Pantheon Books, a division of Random House, Inc. – Ssu-K'ung Shu for "At the Riverside Village" from *The Penguin Book of Chinese Verse*, translated by Robert Kotewall and Norman L. Smith, pub. Penguin Books – Maggie Simmans for "Storms" – Ian Souter for "You Don't Frighten Me" – Pauline Stewart for "Old Songs" and "Garden Zoo" from *Singing Down the Breadfruit*, pub. The Bodley Head Children's Books – Taira Tadanori for "Overtaken by the Dark" from *The Penguin Book of Japanese Verse* edited and translated by Geoffrey Bownas and Anthony Thwaite, pub. Penguin Books – Rabindranath Tagore for "I Wish I Were..." – Sean Taylor for "The Sleep Stealer" – Alan Temperley for "The Lighthouse" – J.R.R. Tolkien for "On the Hearth the Fire is Red" from *The Road Goes On Forever*, pub. HarperCollins Publishers Ltd – James S. Tippett for "Ducks at Dawn" and "Sunning", from *Crickety Cricket! The Best Loved Poems of James S. Tippett*, pub. HarperCollins Publishers – Telcine Turner for "Listen" – Judith Viorst for "Night Fun" from *If I Were In Charge of the World and Other Worries*, pub. Atheneum Books for Young Readers, reproduced by permission of Simon & Schuster, Ashton Scholastic, Lescher & Lescher and AM Heath Ltd – Celia Warren for "Blue Flashing Light" from *Emergency Poems*, pub. OUP, "Night Ride" from *Transport Poems*, pub. OUP, "My Glow in the Dark Bedroom" and "Bedroom Tactics" – Colin West for "The Farmer's Shadow" from *A Moment in Rhyme*, pub. Random Century – David Whitehead for "Witchy Kittens", pub. Scholastic, "Riding on a Giant" pub. OUP and "My Moons" – Ursula Moray Williams for "Communications" and "With a Grandchild" reproduced with permission of Curtis Brown Ltd – David Higham Associates for "The Weeper" by Gina Wilson from *Jim-Jam Pyjamas*, pub. Jonathan Cape – Raymond Wilson for "The Traveller" – Kit Wright for "The Sea in the Trees", "My Dad, Your Dad", "A Poem Just Like This" – W.B. Yeats for "The Song of Wandering Aengus" from Collected Poems – Benjamin Zephaniah for "Over de Moon" from *Talking Turkeys*, pub. Viking.